REMARKABLE
MINDS

REMARKABLE MINDS

*Seventeen More Pioneering Women
in Science and Medicine*

Pendred Noyce

TUMBLEHOME LEARNING, INC.
BOSTON, MASSACHUSETTS

Dedication

To Rhianon, who has always had the courage
and good judgment to follow her own path.

BOOK DESIGN BY JEANNE ABBOUD

Library of Congress Control Number: 2015907841
ISBN: 9781943431137

CONTENTS

FOREWORD

Women have participated in the development of the sciences since the sixteenth century, although their contributions have long gone unacknowledged. Written in an engaging style, this timely text by Pendred Noyce and its predecessor *Magnificent Minds* create a portrait gallery of women who were pioneers in science, engineering, mathematics, and medicine. These volumes deserve the close attention of the education community. Moreover, for anyone seeking insights into a life in science, the recurring patterns that appear throughout these narratives are essential knowledge.

The essays in the two books do not simply recount interesting stories, nor do they offer routine biographies describing women's accomplishments. Instead, women's lives are clearly situated in the context of their time and the society in which they lived. For example, Italy in the eighteenth century did not impose the constraints on women that were commonplace in most other European countries. The lack of opportunities in education for women—in many cases active parental and institutional discouragement—is a theme repeated throughout the accounts and continued into the twentieth century. In the case of published works, many pre-nineteenth-century French women, preferring to remain anonymous or pseudonymous, did not have their names on the title-pages of their works. When writing about the private lives of the women, the author focuses on marriage and family, matters that continue to present concerns for young people who may be considering a career in science.

The women's interactions with the scientific establishments of their times varied from being confined to the role of an independent scholar, working as an unpaid assistant, and in some fortunate cases being mentored in their chosen field. In the end, despite gender bias and other obstacles, the extraordinary women who are the subjects of these two volumes persevered and created their own individual paths to success.

As the curators who organized the 2013 exhibition "Extraordinary Women in Science & Medicine: Four Centuries of Achievement" at the Grolier Club and authored the book of the same title, we hope these volumes by Pendred Noyce will be noticed and read by young people, teachers, and important members of the education community. We are delighted to see our work in its second life and in the service of encouraging education and learning.

RONALD K. SMELTZER
PAULETTE ROSE
ROBERT J. RUBEN

ACKNOWLEDGMENTS

This book, like its predecessor, *Magnificent Minds*, grew out of an exhibition at the Grolier Club in New York. Special thanks go to the three curators of that exhibit. Paulette Rose, who originally conceived of the exhibition, provided invaluable help with everything French. As a young surgical resident, Robert Ruben created an amplified stethoscope to help Helen Taussig with her failing hearing. He kindly reviewed all the medical chapters in this book. Ronald Smeltzer provided extensive feedback, fact-checking, and help locating images. Without the three devoted curators, this book would not exist.

I would also like to thank Steve Rasmussen for introducing me to the exhibition, and Irena and Gene Bonte for supporting the publication of *Magnificent Minds*. Their act of generosity allowed this project to go forward.

As always, I thank my patient and supportive husband, Leo.

INTRODUCTION

From a French noblewoman to the granddaughter of slaves, seventeen women of science and medicine populate the pages of this book. The women grew up in seven countries and pursued their studies in mathematics, chemistry, physics, medicine, and astronomy at different times across more than three centuries. Like the subjects of this book's companion volume, *Magnificent Minds*, the women profiled here were individuals of strong personality who defied stereotypes, yet their stories also share certain themes that make them exemplars worthy of study.

Of the seventeen women in this book, ten were married, seven to fellow scientists. For two of the women, Gerty Cori and Irène Joliot-Curie, their husbands were also their closest scientific collaborators. Almost two-thirds of the women found in the two books married, suggesting that although a number of scientific women over the past four centuries chose science over family life, many found a way to combine the two.

As in *Magnificent Minds*, the scientific careers of the women in this book reveal society's gradual acceptance of the roles that women can play in academia and research. Contemporaries of the five earliest women in this book considered them gifted amateurs. It was only because they were supported by fathers, by husbands, or by inherited wealth that they could afford the luxury of studying science. Indeed, most of these early women hesitated to claim their identity as scientists. Émilie Du Châtelet boldly flouted convention by living openly with her paramour, Voltaire, but she kept her early scientific publications anonymous. Maria Gaetana Agnesi's father arranged for her to be educated in mathematics and philosophy, but rather than take a university position like her contemporary Laura Bassi, Agnesi retired to a life of religious contemplation and good works. Madame Thiroux d'Arconville, equally pious, maintained her anonymity from all but a few close associates throughout her long and prolific life. Sophie Germain, growing up in Revolutionary France, initially posed as a man when she corresponded with her mathematical mentors, although late in life she did win a prestigious mathematics prize in her own name. Of the five women in this book who were active before the eighteenth century, only the English chemist Elizabeth Fulhame boldly proclaimed her identity from the outset, along with her equal right, despite being female, to contribute to scientific knowledge.

Of the later twelve women in this book, all earned income from their work as scientists or physicians. Five of the women were awarded Nobel Prizes for their research. However, even the Nobel laureates were often underpaid compared with their male colleagues. Both Maria Mayer and

Gerty Cori found their careers hampered by institutional anti-nepotism policies: universities that hired their husbands as faculty members declined to hire the wives at any but a token salary. Cecilia Payne Gaposchkin escaped Harvard University's anti-nepotism policy, since she was employed in the astronomy department before her husband-to-be. Still, for many years she was underpaid and barred from the faculty club.

Remarkable Minds features seven Jewish women, of whom two were English, two American, one Austrian, one Italian, and one born in the future Czechoslovakia. Gerty Cori and her husband left Prague for the United States in the 1920s because of anti-Semitism and economic devastation in their home country. Maria Blau fled for Mexico when the Anschluss brought Hitler's followers into power in her native Austria. Rita Levi-Montalcini remained in Italy during World War II. She even managed to continue her research in a clandestine home laboratory until the German invasion led her to flee to Florence and pose as Christian. Once the war was over, though, she left her battered homeland for a six-month fellowship in the United States that stretched into a lifetime appointment. The Jewish women scientists of the United States and England avoided this level of danger and disruption. Although they faced anti-Semitism, either subtle or overt, they voiced indignation over how they were treated as women more often than over how they were treated as Jews.

Only one woman of color, the African American oncologist Jane Cooke Wright, is profiled in *Remarkable Minds*. Features of her biography suggest why she is an exception. Only two generations away from slavery, Wright was nevertheless a member of her family's third generation of doctors. She grew up in a respected middle-class family that placed a high value on education, and her father, a community leader as well as a physician, served her as both role model and mentor. Few African American women of her generation had similar advantages. Today, as opportunities for women of color open more widely, African American women are rising to the upper levels of departments of science and medicine across the country.

One final theme that emerges more strongly in this book than in its predecessor is the theme of women helping women. Hertha Ayrton was the only professed suffragette among the seventeen profiled here; she marched, provided financial support to the suffrage movement, and nursed released hunger strikers back to health in her London home. But several of her fellow scientists and physicians benefited from the growing economic power and philanthropic savvy of women enriched by the Industrial Revolution. Such newly empowered women founded Smith College and negotiated equal treatment of female applicants to Johns Hopkins School of Medicine. Their contributions opened doors for women, and the women who passed through those doors began to advise and advocate for one another. Stick it out, Florence Sabin advised Helen Taussig, and Taussig passed on the advice to women who followed her. When Cecilia Payne Gaposchkin was appointed chair of the department of astronomy at Harvard, she threw a party for all the young women in the department and announced, "I find myself cast in the unlikely role of a thin wedge."

Audience members attending talks on the heroines of *Magnificent Minds* often ask if the climate for women in science has changed. The answer is that the climate has changed enormously. Girls now take virtually the same number of advanced high school science and mathematics courses as boys. Very nearly fifty percent of medical school graduates in the United States are women. To be certain, women have not achieved parity with men across the board. Women make up only about a third of scientific researchers worldwide. They still lag behind men in obtaining physics and computer science degrees, and they are still rare among the ranks of full professors, department chairs, and deans. Women students in heavily male science departments may still encounter ignorant assumptions about their abilities and interests; they may endure sexist attitudes and comments; and they may still suffer from policies unfriendly to the demands of raising a family. But with a little searching, women in science today are able to find peers and female mentors. They have more equitable access to education and advancement than ever before in history. If the women in this book could achieve at the highest levels of science despite educational disparities, financial difficulties, wartime disruptions, institutional biases, and social upheaval, then there is all the more reason for young women of today to strive for and celebrate the achievements of their own remarkable minds.

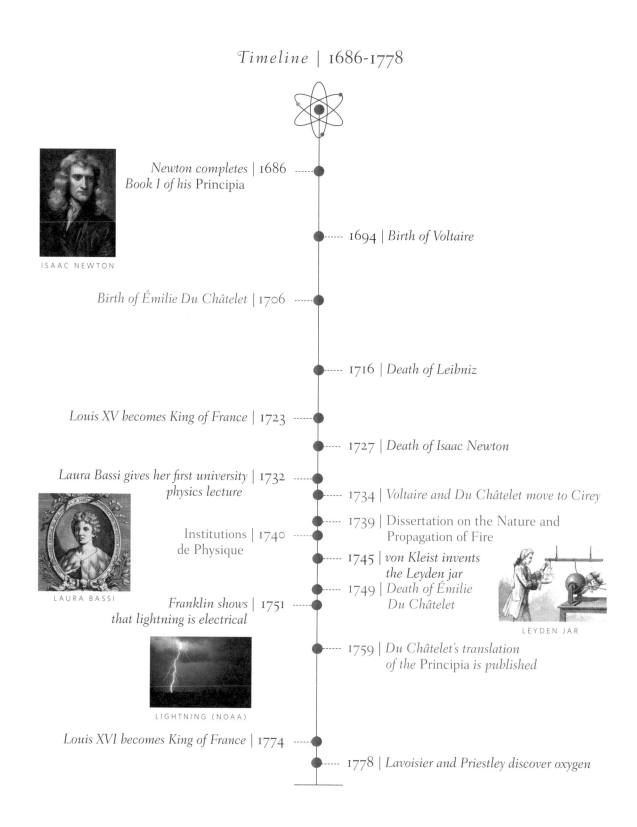

Timeline | 1686-1778

ISAAC NEWTON

Newton completes | 1686
Book I of his Principia

1694 | Birth of Voltaire

Birth of Émilie Du Châtelet | 1706

1716 | Death of Leibniz

Louis XV becomes King of France | 1723

1727 | Death of Isaac Newton

Laura Bassi gives her first university | 1732
physics lecture

1734 | Voltaire and Du Châtelet move to Cirey

1739 | Dissertation on the Nature and
Propagation of Fire

Institutions | 1740
de Physique

1745 | von Kleist invents
the Leyden jar

LAURA BASSI

1749 | Death of Émilie
Du Châtelet

Franklin shows | 1751
that lightning is electrical

LEYDEN JAR

1759 | Du Châtelet's translation
of the Principia is published

LIGHTNING (NOAA)

Louis XVI becomes King of France | 1774

1778 | Lavoisier and Priestley discover oxygen

1 | *Fire and Living Force*

Émilie Du Châtelet

1706-1749 | *France*

Gabrielle-Émilie le Tonnelier de Breteuil, scholar and woman of society, was born to the lesser nobility during the reign of King Louis XIV. Her father held the post of master of protocol, instructing visiting ambassadors in how to approach the king.

Little is known for certain about Émilie's early education. Her parents appear to have encouraged her by respecting her mind. A visitor noted how she impertinently questioned her mother. To the visitor's surprise, she received answers instead of the shushing a well-brought-up child might expect. As an adult, Émilie was fluent in Latin and read widely in multiple languages.

"Truthfully, Madame Du Châtelet is a prodigy."
- Voltaire

At age eighteen, Émilie married a colonel in one of the king's regiments. Florent-Claude, Marquis Du Châtelet, was twelve years older than Émilie. As a marquis, Du Châtelet far outranked his new wife's family, but in material wealth he brought to the marriage only a chateau in shabby condition and its accompanying fields and forests. Though frequently away on military campaigns, Florent-Claude proved to be a devoted and tolerant husband, remaining supportive of Émilie in all her endeavors and even accepting her romantic entanglements with other men during his long absences.

ÉMILIE DU CHÂTELET

During the early years of their marriage, Émilie bore Florent-Claude two sons, one of whom died in infancy and the other of whom later lost his head in the French revolution. She also had a daughter, who eventually married into the royal family of Naples, after which she never saw her mother again. The family spent much of their time in Paris, where Madame Du Châtelet maintained a household of about twenty servants and two carriages. Because their modest income from Florent-Claude's military pay and the lands and iron forges at his estate in Cirey could not support her extravagance, Du Châtelet constantly borrowed money.

During her early twenties, the marquise immersed herself in the frivolity and intrigue of life at court. Powdering her hair and lightly rouging her pale face, she prepared for the day. Wearing one of her thirty outfits, with skirts and corsets, sleeves that could be sewn on or removed, ribbons, lace, and gauze, she rode through the streets borne by servants in a sedan chair lined in crimson velvet. At the court of the new king, Louis XV, she gambled at cards and ate and drank with friends. Evenings at the opera or theater were followed by social gatherings for gossip and amusement that could last into the small hours.

At about age twenty-six, however, Émilie Du Châtelet found a group of friends with more intellectual interests. Deciding to challenge herself by studying mathematics, she convinced an honored member of the Royal Academy of Sciences, Pierre-Louis Moreau de Maupertuis, and his young protégé Alexis Claude Clairaut, to tutor her in algebra and geometry. In a portrait painted at the time, the young marquise, dressed in brocade, fur, and lace, holds a book in one hand and a sheet of geometric drawings in the other.

In the same year, Émilie became entranced by the poet and playwright François-Marie Arouet, universally known as Voltaire. Twelve years older than the marquise and of much lower rank, Voltaire was small and slight, with a quick wit

MAUPERTUIS

and a lively way with words. His reckless rhymes and gift for satire often got him in trouble with the French government. By the time he and Émilie met, his father had disinherited him, he had fled into exile more than once, and he had twice served time in France's most feared prison, the Bastille. Nevertheless, he was already recognized as France's most prominent writer.

The Bastille St. Antoine *was a French fortress built in Paris in the fourteenth century. In 1417 it was declared a state prison, and it played a role in most domestic French conflicts thereafter. Louis XIV used it to imprison members of the nobility who had angered him, along with French Protestants after the king revoked the Edict of Nantes. Under later kings, the Bastille imprisoned men of more varied social backgrounds, often including writers who fell afoul of the king's censors. Although they were relatively well treated, these writers often wrote accounts of their captivity that angered the public. On July 14, 1789, a revolutionary mob stormed the Bastille, murdered its governor, and released the seven remaining prisoners. The event marked the start of the French Revolution, and July 14th is still celebrated in France as Bastille Day, a national holiday.*

VOLTAIRE, BY NICOLAS DE LARGILLIÈRE

Voltaire was astonished to find in Émilie not only beauty but a mind whose quickness matched and even surpassed his own. He wrote to a friend that she learned English in fifteen days so they could read the English philosopher John Locke together. In mathematics, she quickly left him behind. "Truthfully," he wrote to a friend, "Madame Du Châtelet is a prodigy."

Before long, Voltaire was courting Du Châtelet, writing poems and complaining that when he wished to talk of love, she wanted only to discuss mathematics and philosophy. Cleverly, he enlisted her in research for a play he was writing. This sign of respect for her intellect may have been more seductive than all his poetry and pleading.

CIREY

In 1734, publication of Voltaire's *Lettres Philosphiques*, drawn from his understanding of English thought and government, led the royal censor to issue a warrant for his arrest. The royal executioner tore up and publicly burned a copy of the *Lettres*, while Voltaire fled to the country estates of one friend after another. Du Châtelet, terrified at the thought of what another stint in prison would do to her friend's fragile health, made a momentous decision. She would abandon Paris and shelter Voltaire in the chateau at Cirey. Her ever tolerant husband agreed and even arranged for the public censor to change Voltaire's sentence to house arrest at Cirey. In return, Voltaire devoted some of the fortune earned through his writings to renovating the chateau.

Thus began an idyllic time for Du Châtelet. By now she was Voltaire's paramour, and despite future affairs for both of them, they remained devoted companions until her death fifteen years later. Together they lived a life of study, conversation, and writing. Philosophers, mathematicians and poets visited them to join in mornings of study and evenings of reading aloud or acting in amateur theatrical performances.

At first, Du Châtelet saw her role as Voltaire's muse. She admired him profoundly, calling him a "metaphysician, a historian, a great philosopher, but one who preferred to be a poet, and thus was known as France's greatest poet." Her role, as she saw it, was "removing the thorns that slow the true geniuses in their course." As for Voltaire, he called Émilie "the most beautiful soul in the world." She read literature and philosophy with him, helped him with research for his plays, and served as his first reader and critic. Du Châtelet was happy.

Voltaire encouraged Du Châtelet in her first independent scholarly work, her translation of Mandeville's *Fable of the Bees* from English into French. Hers was a very free translation, interspersed with her own reflections on the writer's theories about the origins of virtue.

Between 1735 and 1737, Du Châtelet studied Newton's *Principia* in English and helped Voltaire write his *Elements of Newton's Philosophy*. Together they read astronomy and physics. With her mathematical background and quick understanding, Du Châtelet helped Voltaire with the fundamentals of Newton's physics. Whole paragraphs of her writing ended up in the book, especially in the sections on color and comets. Although Du Châtelet's name does not appear on the title page, Voltaire considered her his co-author. Referring to Du Châtelet as the Roman goddess Minerva in a 1737 letter to Frederick the Great, Voltaire wrote, "Minerva dictated and I wrote." Voltaire designed the book's frontispiece, where he sits writing while Newton shines a light in the heavens above. Du Châtelet hovers in the air a little to one side, holding up a mirror that gathers light from Newton and reflects it to Voltaire laboring below.

Craving recognition as a scientist, Voltaire next decided to enter the Academy of Science's prize competition for essays on the nature of fire. This time, instead of just quoting the authorities, Voltaire decided to carry out experiments of his own. He and Du Châtelet turned to the forges of Cirey. They weighed iron and measured its volume, melted it, let it harden, and weighed and measured it again. Iron that had been heated and cooled weighed the same and had the same nature as when they started, but lead treated the same way changed into a pile of white powder that had increased in weight. Neither substance lost weight in the fire. How could it be true, then, as Newton said, that fire had mass of its own?

As the deadline for submission of the competition essays approached, Du Châtelet realized that she could not agree with Voltaire's interpretation of their experiments. She disagreed with Voltaire's beloved Newton that fire, light, and matter all had the same nature. With two weeks to go, she decided to write her own essay in secret. In the essay, she suggested, among other ideas, that different colors of light carry different amounts of heat. In 1800, the scientist William Herschel actually carried out an experiment demonstrating that heat carried by light increases across the spectrum from violet to red.

Du Châtelet's loyal husband submitted her essay for her anonymously so as to conceal the author's gender. In the end, though neither Du Châtelet nor Voltaire won one of the three prizes, the examiners thought highly enough of their entries to publish both along with those of the three winners. Du Châtelet's essay seems to have been the first paper written by a woman to be published by the French Academy of Sciences.

FRONTISPIECE OF VOLTAIRE'S *ELEMENTS OF NEWTON'S PHILOSOPHY*

In developing her conception of force vive *or* **living force**, *Émilie Du Châtelet repeated the experiments of a Dutch natural philosopher named Willem Jacob 's Gravesande. The experiments consisted of dropping brass balls from increasing heights onto soft clay. As Du Châtelet increased the height from which the balls were dropped, their speed also increased. 's Gravesande's key observation, which Du Châtelet reproduced, was that the depth of the impression the balls made in clay increased proportionally with their speed squared. In fact, what the experiment measured was kinetic energy, which we now know to be ½ times mass times velocity squared.*

Now that learned men were taking her seriously as a scholar, Du Châtelet delved deeper into physics. When her ten-year-old son's tutor proved inept, Du Châtelet took over the boy's education. She decided to write him a book explaining the workings of physics. Illustrations at the beginnings of her chapters show men engaged in activities that could demonstrate optics or the laws of motion: blowing bubbles, throwing a ball, balancing on a seesaw, watching a billiard ball rebound off a wall, or shooting a gun. She titled her book *Institutions de physique*, or *The Foundations of Physics*.

As she was working on her physics book, Du Châtelet decided she wanted to learn calculus, although the book itself contains no mathematics. This time she worked with a young mathematician named Samuel König. As the book became more complex, Du Châtelet debated the competing ideas of Newton, Leibniz, and others and worked to synthesize them. König later tried to claim that all the ideas in her book were his own, but few people paid him any attention.

The *Institutions* was well received. However, the secretary of the Academy of Sciences, Dortous de Mairan, published a pamphlet in which he mockingly disputed Du Châtelet's formulation of *force vive* in the last chapter of her book. Force, he argued, was mass times velocity, not mass times velocity squared. Du Châtelet answered Mairan point by point in a pamphlet of her own. Most readers judged her the winner of the argument. Here she was, a noblewoman outside the Academy, successfully debating an established scholar. Neither formula for *force vive* corresponds with our current understanding of force as mass times acceleration: Mairan's formulation corresponds to the magnitude of momentum, while Du Châtelet's approaches our formulation of kinetic energy.

For her next project, Du Châtelet wrote a seven hundred-page critique of the Bible, pointing out its cruelties and inconsistencies. Too sensible ever to publish such a work, she merely circulated it among her scholarly friends.

In 1745, at the age of thirty-nine, Du Châtelet took on her chef-d'oeuvre: a translation of Newton's *Principia* into French. She included an addendum to explain its mathematics, and she wrote 279 pages of commentary on its ideas. In giving examples of how Newton's principles could be applied to problems, she demonstrated the use of calculus, although Newton himself had avoided using it in the *Principia*. The work took Du Châtelet four years to complete. Even as she worked on the book, she wrote a more autobiographical piece, a *Discourse on Happiness*. Among the sources of happiness she described, such as food, gambling, and love, she mentioned study, especially for women. She noted that although many routes to glory, such as politics and military prowess, are closed to them, women can find renown as scholars.

> *"I finish it for reason and for honor."*

By this time Voltaire, although still living with Du Châtelet as an intellectual companion, had begun an affair with his widowed niece. In 1748, Du Châtelet, too, fell in love, this time with a young army captain and poet named Jean-Francois de Saint-Lambert. Within a few months, Du Châtelet found herself pregnant by Lambert. Du Châtelet was over forty years old, and the pregnancy filled her with foreboding. In the face of her fears, she redoubled her efforts to finish her translation of the *Principia*. Though she loved him, she told Lambert, she could not join him until her book was finished. "I finish it for reason and for honor," she wrote. Each day she rose at eight or nine to write, continuing with only the shortest breaks for nourishment or conversation until she fell into bed at five in the morning.

Toward the end of August 1749, Du Châtelet put down her quill with the book complete. A week later she gave birth to a daughter, apparently without difficulty. Ten days later she was dead. Voltaire wrote a eulogy for her, calling her a "great friend and great man," while Lambert wept every day for months. As for her husband the marquis, he never remarried.

Despite Du Châtelet's fierce devotion to her work, her translation of Newton's *Principia* was not published for another ten years. Today it is still the only French translation of Newton's masterpiece. Laura Bassi probably used the 1743 Italian translation of Du Châtelet's book *Institutions* in her physics course at Bologna. Along with Voltaire, Du Châtelet can be credited with first bringing Newton's ideas to wide notice in France.

During her lifetime, the Marquise Du Châtelet overcame mockery and doubt to achieve the respect her scholarship deserved. After her death, however, lesser men sometimes claimed her work as their own, and for several centuries she was remembered more as Voltaire's passionate and often foolish muse than as a scholar in her own right. Only in recent decades has she been widely recognized for her role as the first woman of physics in France.

Timeline | 1718-1799

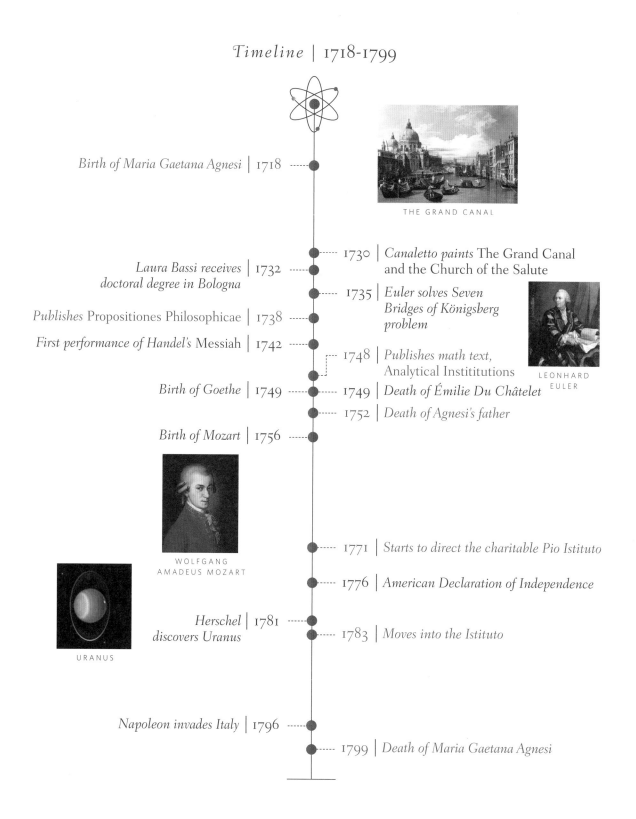

Birth of Maria Gaetana Agnesi | 1718

THE GRAND CANAL

1730 | Canaletto paints The Grand Canal and the Church of the Salute

Laura Bassi receives | 1732
doctoral degree in Bologna

1735 | Euler solves Seven Bridges of Königsberg problem

Publishes Propositiones Philosophicae | 1738

First performance of Handel's Messiah | 1742

1748 | Publishes math text, Analytical Instititutions

Birth of Goethe | 1749

1749 | Death of Émilie Du Châtelet

LEONHARD EULER

1752 | Death of Agnesi's father

Birth of Mozart | 1756

WOLFGANG AMADEUS MOZART

1771 | Starts to direct the charitable Pio Istituto

1776 | American Declaration of Independence

Herschel | 1781
discovers Uranus

1783 | Moves into the Istituto

URANUS

Napoleon invades Italy | 1796

1799 | Death of Maria Gaetana Agnesi

2 | *Reluctant Prodigy*

Maria Gaetana Agnesi

1718-1799 | *Italy*

MARIA GAETANA AGNESI

In 1745, a wealthy silk merchant named Pietro Agnesi installed a printing press in his Milan mansion so his twenty-seven-year-old daughter could supervise the printing of her new calculus textbook. The daughter, Maria Gaetana Agnesi, instructed the printer on how to represent equations and mathematical symbols. Some of the equations were so long and complicated they had to be printed on large sheets of paper that could be folded to fit between pages. With the printing, Agnesi became the first woman to author and supervise the printing of a book of advanced mathematics.

Maria Gaetani Agnesi was born on May 16, 1718, the first of her father's twenty-one children by three wives. Like Laura Bassi, Italy's first female physicist and professor, she was recognized as a prodigy from an early age. Her doting and ambitious father saw that she learned Greek, Latin, and Hebrew as well as French and other modern languages. Maria Gaetana was nine years

The 1700s in Italy are known as the **Settecento**. *Politically, the Italian city-states were divided, with some independent, some ruled by Spain or Austria, and some under the Pope's direct rule. Culturally, the Renaissance had ended, and the Counter-Reformation was coming to an end. Scholarship advanced in the great universities. Large sculpture continued in the Baroque tradition: the Trevi Fountain was completed in 1762 after thirty years of work. Architecture and smaller sculpture developed into the even more ornate Rococo style. Carlo Goldoni, author of over 150 comedies, was the best-known author, and Antonio Vivaldi the most important composer.*

old when she made her first scholarly public appearance. In front of a group of Milanese nobles, she presented in perfect Latin an argument in favor of educating women. The essay itself was probably written by one of her tutors, but two years later, the text was published, and the young Agnesi became well known.

Having famous daughters was just what Pietro wanted. He identified his second daughter, Maria Teresa, as the musically talented one, and she became a polished harpsichordist and composer whose pieces are still played today. From their early teens, both girls performed at cultural evenings at home, arranged by their father. A French visitor, Charles de Brosses, described one of these evenings:

> *I was brought into a large fine room, where I found about thirty people from all countries of Europe, arranged in a circle and Mlle Agnesi, all alone with her little sister, seated on a sofa. She is a girl of about twenty years of age, neither ugly nor pretty, with a very simple and very sweet manner . . . Count Belloni . . . began with a fine discourse in Latin to this young girl, that it might be understood by all. She answered him well, after which they entered into a dispute, in the same language, on the origin of fountains and on the causes of the ebb and flow which is seen in some of them, similar to tides at sea. She spoke like an angel on this topic, I have never heard anything so pleasurable . . .*

Pleasurable as these evenings were to visitors, Maria Gaetana found them onerous. She felt certain that for every listener who enjoyed hearing her defend some thesis, another nineteen found themselves terribly bored.

"She spoke like an angel . . ."

At age twenty, Agnesi published *Propositiones Philosophicae*. These were 191 theses on philosophy and natural science, based on her public discussions. Like Laura Bassi, Agnesi supported the "moderns" against the "scholastics" and was especially interested in Newton's theories about physics. By this time, her public performances made her increasingly unhappy. She liked to study, and her new study of mathematics especially delighted her, but she disliked public display. By nature shy and pious, she would much rather retire from public view and devote herself to good works.

> "... *sustained by the strongest inclination toward mathematics* ..."

Finally, at the age of twenty-one, Agnesi told her father she wished to enter a convent and become a nun. Horrified, he negotiated a compromise. Maria would continue to live at home, doing charitable works, studying mathematics, and managing the household and her numerous siblings. In return, she could dress simply and attend church whenever she chose. Her father would not ask her to attend balls, the theater, or other "profane amusements."

Freed from public display, the young Agnesi devoted herself to religion and mathematics. Her room was filled with treatises and mathematical instruments. To learn calculus, she studied books and papers in different languages. Luckily, a monk named Ramiro Rampinelli, who was also a mathematician, willingly helped her work through the most difficult equations. Agnesi wrote, "With all the study, sustained by the strongest inclination towards mathematics, that I forced myself to devote to it on my own, I should have become altogether tangled," if not for Rampinelli's help.

Before long, Rampinelli suggested that Agnesi write a textbook of her own. Perhaps initially intended as a guide for her younger brothers, the book grew to be much more. Agnesi wrote in the Tuscan dialect of Italian, not her native Milanese dialect, which suggests she was seeking a broad audience. She called the book *Instituzioni Analitiche* or *Analytical Institutions*, and it covered algebra, geometry, calculus, and elementary differential equations. Agnesi asked other mathematicians to review the book before she printed it. During the printing, she paid special attention to fifty-eight folding plates illustrating curves in two dimensions. When the book finally

RAMIRO RAMPINELLI

MATHEMATICS

Agnesi was fascinated by mathematical curves. One hill-shaped curve she studied had first been described by Fermat and then Grandi, who named it versiera, *a word derived from the Latin* vertere, *to turn. When Cambridge professor John Colson translated Agnesi's textbook in 1801, he misread* la versiera *as* l'avversiera, *which means wife of the devil, or witch. Because of Colson's mistranslation, a curve became a witch, and casual readers may think of the saintly Maria Gaetana as the* **Witch of Agnesi.** *Here is the Witch of Agnesi curve, from Wikimedia Commons. For an animation of its construction, visit: http://mathworld.wolfram.com/ WitchofAgnesi.html*

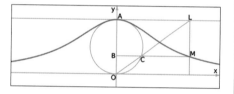

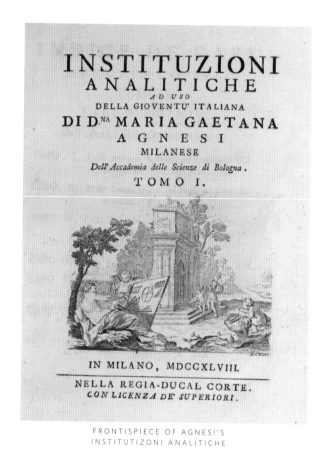

FRONTISPIECE OF AGNESI'S
INSTITUTIZONI ANALITICHE

appeared in 1748, Agnesi dedicated the finished product to Empress Maria Theresa.

Analytical Institutions was very well received. The book had managed to present in a coherent progression the discoveries of mathematicians who used different approaches, languages, methods, and even notation. A review from the Academy of Sciences in Paris stated, "Order, clarity and precision reign in all parts of this work." Empress Maria Theresa sent a diamond ring and a small crystal casket encrusted with precious stones. From Bologna, Laura Bassi wrote a letter of congratulations. Pope Benedict XIV, the same pope who had helped Laura Bassi advance, arranged for Agnesi to be appointed to a chair of mathematics at the University of Bologna.

However, the retiring Agnesi never took up her professorship. She never even left Milan. When their father died in 1752, both of the elder Agnesi daughters, who had patiently obeyed their father for so many years, finally followed their own wishes. While her younger sister married a man she had long loved, Maria Gaetana withdrew from public life and devoted herself to charity.

". . . an angel of consolation to the sick and dying women. . . ."

She taught poor girls and opened her father's house to "the poor and suffering, the hopelessly ill and the demented." She also visited patients in the city hospital. When in 1771 Milan opened a new charitable home called the *Pio Istituto Trivulzio*, the archbishop asked Agnesi to direct it. This appointment she accepted. To fund her charitable work, she skimped on dresses, meals, even books and her gifts from the Empress. Then, in 1783, Agnesi herself moved into the Institute. The official records of the Pio Istituto remember her as "an angel of consolation to the sick and dying women." She died at the Istituto at the age of 81 and was buried with other residents in a common grave.

Maria Gaetana Agnesi was only thirty-four when she gave up mathematics for good. While many of the women in this book had to overcome parental objections to pursue their studies, Agnesi seems to have been the opposite: a gifted young girl whose proud and well-meaning father pushed her onto a public stage too early and too eagerly. Although she loved mathematics—she could never have mastered it so well if she had not—she felt herself drawn most strongly to a life of pious charity.

Agnesi did not make original mathematical discoveries. Her strength lay in interpreting, organizing, and making accessible the work of others. Agnesi filled her book with examples rather than theory. *Analytical Institutions* presented the most advanced mathematics of its time in a way young scholars could understand, while her own example proved that women could master advanced mathematics.

MARIA GAETANA AGNESI WHEN SHE WAS OLDER

Timeline | 1706-1805

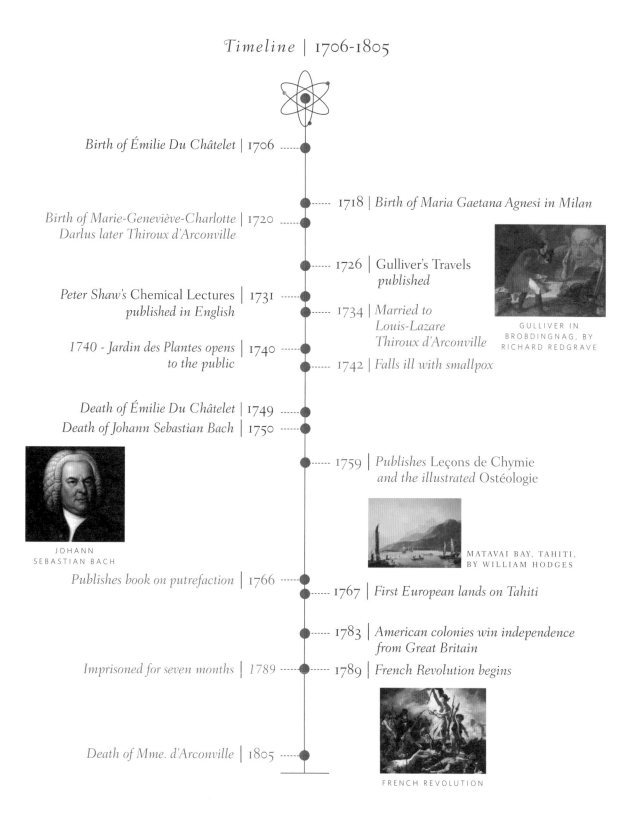

Birth of Émilie Du Châtelet | 1706

1718 | Birth of Maria Gaetana Agnesi in Milan

Birth of Marie-Geneviève-Charlotte | 1720
Darlus later Thiroux d'Arconville

1726 | Gulliver's Travels
published

Peter Shaw's Chemical Lectures | 1731
published in English

1734 | Married to
Louis-Lazare
Thiroux d'Arconville

GULLIVER IN
BROBDINGNAG, BY
RICHARD REDGRAVE

1740 - Jardin des Plantes opens | 1740
to the public

1742 | Falls ill with smallpox

Death of Émilie Du Châtelet | 1749
Death of Johann Sebastian Bach | 1750

1759 | Publishes Leçons de Chymie
and the illustrated Ostéologie

JOHANN
SEBASTIAN BACH

MATAVAI BAY, TAHITI,
BY WILLIAM HODGES

Publishes book on putrefaction | 1766

1767 | First European lands on Tahiti

1783 | American colonies win independence
from Great Britain

Imprisoned for seven months | 1789

1789 | French Revolution begins

Death of Mme. d'Arconville | 1805

FRENCH REVOLUTION

3 | *Flesh and Bones*

Marie-Geneviève-Charlotte Thiroux d'Arconville

1720-1805 | *France*

Marie-Geneviève-Charlotte Thiroux d'Arconville was a woman of wide-ranging talent and knowledge who made contributions as a scientist, biographer, historian, novelist, essayist, and translator. But despite the breadth of her scholarship, she has never been well known, primarily because she wrote anonymously. As a pious woman and member of an aristocratic family, she wanted to avoid the criticism and mockery that so often seemed to befall any woman claiming an intellectual life. Self-taught and voracious for knowledge, she sought primarily to be useful and to occupy her restless mind. Her authorship was known to a small circle of scientists who respected her work, but broader fame was apparently never important to her.

Born in 1720, Marie-Geneviève-Charlotte was only fourteen years younger than Émilie Du Châtelet. She was born in Paris to the Darlus family; her father was a wealthy farmer-general, or

MADEMOISELLE DARLUS,
BY CHARLES-ANTOINE COYPEL, 1735

LOUIS MANDRIN, SMUGGLER AND REBEL
AGAINST THE TAX FARMING SYSTEM, 1755

Tax farmers *in France before the
Revolution bought the right to collect and
keep taxes owed to the state. The state
received a fixed, assured revenue; while
the farmers took the risk and received
the benefit of whatever taxes they could
collect. Tax farmers were wealthy but not
well-loved by the people.*

tax farmer. Marie-Geneviève-Charlotte lost her mother
at the age of four, and her schooling was turned over to
a series of governesses. Her education was shockingly
lopsided. She disliked her music teacher, and her dancing instructor failed to inspire her. She was introduced
both to painting and to sculpture, which she loved. But
she was taught no languages, science, or mathematics.
She did not learn to write until she was eight years old,
but once she picked up the pen she seldom set it down.
She wrote dozens of books and told friends later in life
that she scarcely had an idea without a pen in her hand.

At age fourteen, by her own request, the young
Darlus daughter was married to another tax farmer,
Louis-Lazare Thiroux d'Arconville. Louis-Lazare later
became a president in the *Parlement* of Paris, a kind of
regional court of justice. Before Thiroux d'Arconville was
twenty, the couple had three sons, the eldest of whom
lost his head in the French Revolution.

As a young wife, Thiroux d'Arconville participated
in the amusements of her class. She especially loved
the theater and opera. But at age twenty-two she suffered a case of smallpox that almost killed her and left
her face badly scarred. Thereafter, whether due to her
close encounter with death or the loss of her beauty, she
withdrew from society and devoted herself to study and
religion. She took on the sober clothing and hairstyle of
a woman of seventy, and turning her thoughts to charity,
she founded a free clinic for the poor near her country
home in Meudon. Then d'Arconville set to work educating herself. At home she studied English and Italian,
and she attended classes at the royal *Jardin des Plantes*,
the King's Garden in Paris, to learn about the sciences.

The *Jardin des Plantes*, which opened to the public in
1640, was a remarkable Enlightenment institution dedicated to gathering and disseminating knowledge. Inside
a seventy-acre park full of botanical specimens were
located three public buildings: a natural history museum,
a chemical laboratory, and an anatomical amphitheater.
Hundreds of people, both men and women, attended
lectures on physics, anatomy, botany, and chemistry in

JARDIN DES PLANTES

the Garden. For the anatomy course, which lasted three months, lecturers dissected twenty cadavers in the amphitheater. The chemistry course consisted of thirty-eight lecture-demonstrations that began at six o'clock every morning. Thiroux d'Arconville probably attended a full course of both chemistry and anatomy.

Up to this point, d'Arconville's actions were not terribly unusual. Many aristocratic women dabbled in science as an amusement, especially botany, and some became collectors of various natural specimens. D'Arconville herself collected rare plants and stones, but that wasn't enough for her. She wanted to learn more. Luckily, she had access to the king's library, from which she had books and papers delivered to her Paris home. In her country home, she built a laboratory and stocked it with simple chemistry equipment. Although she avoided the entertainments of society in general, she did host a salon of sorts to which she regularly invited botanists, chemists, and writers.

For a while, d'Arconville tried her hand at botany, and there are records of her sending specimens to the *Jardin des Plantes*, but her scientific interests eventually turned to chemistry. She worked under the guidance of Jean-Pierre Macquer, professor of chemistry and pharmacology at the *Jardin des Plantes*. In 1759, Macquer encouraged her to translate Peter Shaw's *Chemical Lectures* (1731) into French.

In the eighteenth century, translation offered a way for women to try their hand at scholarship by delving deeply into a subject and presenting it to others, often with accompanying commentary. Three years earlier, d'Arconville had already translated the Marquis of Halifax George Savile's

Advice from a Father to His Daughter. In the preface of that book she bemoaned the fact that rearing daughters was often left to unqualified governesses or nuns because mothers themselves could not be bothered to assume that responsibility.

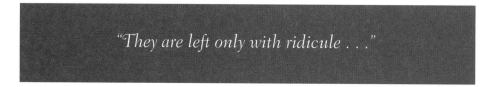

"They are left only with ridicule . . ."

Already d'Arconville had made the decision that her works would remain anonymous before all but a few close associates. Later, in an essay on women, she wrote, "Do they show science or wit? If their works are bad, they are jeered at; if they are good, they are taken from them, and they are left only with ridicule for letting themselves be called authors."

Like Du Châtelet in her study of Newton, d'Arconville did more than translate Shaw's chemistry text. She added a ninety-page introduction explaining the history of practical chemistry, beginning with the earliest days and progressing through Egypt and the ancient world to current times. With frequent references to the work of other scholars, she demonstrated a broad knowledge of her subject. She was also quick to correct what she perceived as errors in other chemists' work, including in Shaw's. Thiroux d'Arconville's translation, titled *Leçons de Chymie Propres a Perfectionner la Physique, la Commerce, et les Arts,* appeared anonymously in 1759.

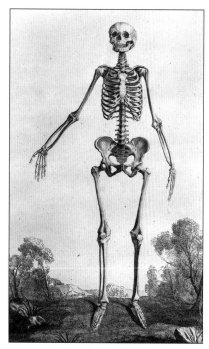

FEMALE SKELETON IN
D'ARCONVILLE'S OSTÉOLOGIE

So prolific and diligent was d'Arconville that she seldom confined herself to one writing project at a time. Subject to insomnia and easily bored, she needed to keep busy. While still working on the chemistry text, she also immersed herself in another task, translating Alexander Monro's *Anatomy of the Human Bones,* which had been published in England in 1729.

To publish her *Ostéologie* or book on bones, d'Arconville sought the help and protection of Jean-Joseph Sue, a professor of anatomy in the royal schools of both surgery and painting as well as royal censor for books of surgery. D'Arconville reorganized the text and added commentaries and a long preface. She also made one great improvement to Monro's treatise: she introduced illustrations. Monro had stated his belief that anatomical illustrations are necessarily inaccurate and should not be used. Although d'Arconville agreed that observation from life is always better, she thought illustration could help with learning; moreover, she wanted to create something beautiful. Looking at well-drawn illustrations, she opined, could help the observer overcome a feeling of

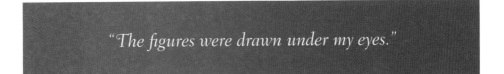

"The figures were drawn under my eyes."

repugnance that would come with looking at such "hideous" things as skeletons. The actual images were most likely created in the studio of d'Arconville's collaborator, Jean-Joseph Sue. Certainly d'Arconville financed them. "The figures were drawn under my eyes," she wrote, "and there were many that I had re-done several times to correct a slight fault."

Thirty-one meticulously printed plates resulted. One of the most remarkable among them was the book's rendition of a female skeleton. The skeleton had a large, broad pelvis, made to look even broader by the narrowness of the lower ribs, which may have been deformed by tight cor-

sets worn by the subject throughout life. However, Thiroux d'Arconville's female skeleton also had a head that was smaller in relation to her other bones than a man's skull would be. In actual fact, it is the other way around: women's skulls are relatively larger compared to the rest of their bodies than are men's skulls. How d'Arconville fell prey to this mistake is not known.

The book itself, when it appeared, was large, heavy, and expensive, far from the handbook for students that Monro had cre-ated. As with her other works, d'Ar-

ALCHEMIST'S IMAGE OF PUTREFACTION, 1678

conville sought to keep her contribution anonymous. As a result, Sue's name appeared alone on the book's title page, and most people naturally assumed he was both translator and artist. He was highly praised for the volume.

Even as she worked on these translation projects, d'Arconville began to pursue independent research of her own. She settled on an unusual project, the study of putrefaction, or how plant and animal matter rot. Her initial work was inspired by studies performed by an English military doctor, John Pringle, who had tried to investigate why some wounds remain healthy while others lead to gangrene.

To d'Arconville, the secret of putrefaction lay at the foundation of chemistry and medicine: how is matter transformed? Over the course of ten years, she carefully recorded 317 experiments with rotting meat, fish, milk, and eggs, treating the foods in various ways to see how putrefaction might

All living things decompose after death. The early stages occur as cells die and release enzymes into surrounding tissue. A later stage, called **putrefaction***, involves the action of bacteria and fungi. In particular, anaerobic bacteria digest the proteins of dead animal tissue and release gases and foul-smelling organic compounds. Nowadays, to slow down this process of rotting, we work to minimize bacterial growth through freezing, wrapping, or preserving meat with salt or other preservatives. The role of bacteria in decomposition and spoilage of food was not understood until Louis Pasteur established the germ theory in the nineteenth century.*

be delayed. For each experiment she noted the weather, sunlight, and humidity. Her major finding was that to preserve food, one must protect it from air. She also confirmed the value of copper, camphor, and cinchona, derived from the bark of an Andean tree, as antiseptic substances that slowed rotting. On the other hand, she differed with John Pringle on the value of chamomile. He had found that it slowed rotting; she disagreed, demonstrating that she had enough confidence in her own research to contradict an authority.

". . . a highly distinguished physician."

Thiroux d'Arconville's studies on putrefaction were published in 1766, once more anonymously, though in the front matter she identified herself as the author of the translation of Shaw's lectures on chemistry. One reviewer praised the writer as obviously a "highly distinguished physician" with a deep knowledge of both chemistry and medicine. The reviewer further urged the writer to reveal "his" identity, but concluded that "he" must be more interested in serving fellow citizens than in burnishing a brilliant reputation.

After 1766, d'Arconville wrote no more original scientific works. The death of a much-loved brother-in-law, her husband's older brother, left her unable to write for a period. She sold her country house with its laboratory, and devoted her time increasingly to the study of history. Eventually she managed to work by dictating to a copyist. In her histories she often compared the present to the past or set up a dialogue between important personages of different eras, such as the cardinals Richelieu and Mazarin. While working on history she continued to write and translate novels and moral essays. She also continued to befriend and correspond with male scholars.

D'Arconville disapproved of most of the philosophers of the Enlightenment. She liked Voltaire's plays but detested his morals. The rise of the Revolution horrified her. In 1789, the year the Bastille fell, her husband died, and d'Arconville was first placed under house arrest and then imprisoned with her family. In short order, her oldest son and her remaining brother-in-law were executed. Surrounded by her sister, her sister-in-law, and her grandson, d'Arconville prepared herself for death. Only the fall of Robespierre saved her; six months after her son's execution she was released. Her investments had melted away, and her younger sons, when they returned from exile, needed her help. When d'Arconville took up her pen once more in 1801, at the age of eighty, it was to try to make sense of her own experience in a collection of "thoughts, reflections, and anecdotes."

MME. THIROUX D'ARCONVILLE

The life of Marie-Geneviève-Charlotte Thiroux d'Arconville demonstrates some of the contradictions of a woman living a scholar's life during the French Enlightenment. Comparison with Émilie Du Châtelet is telling. Both turned away from their prescribed roles as society women in order to educate themselves and use their minds. Both established their writing careers with essay writing and translation. Both were driven to keep writing to the end of their lives. But d'Arconville was much more conventional than Du Châtelet. She embraced religion, and she abided by the eighteenth century code of behavior regarding her role as wife and mother. Although perfectly willing to critique another scholar's work, she shied away from social controversy, and so maintained her lifelong anonymity before all but a few colleagues. Her closest friends and colleagues were men. No feminist, she thought that most women wasted their lives on frivolity, although she also sympathized with their hard lot and the gaps in their education.

Thiroux d'Arconville's experiments on putrefaction continued to be known and cited throughout the first half of the nineteenth century, when an understanding of germs and microbes eclipsed their importance. For most of two centuries, the rest of her work and her very name were little known even to students of Enlightenment France. Only in 2011 did a full volume of intellectual history and criticism devoted to her work appear in France.

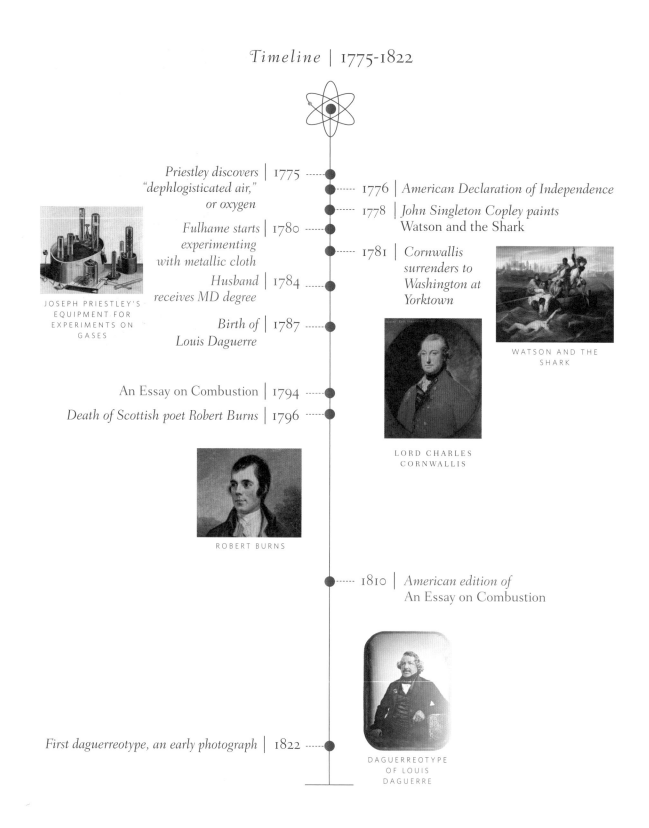

Timeline | 1775-1822

Priestley discovers | 1775
"dephlogisticated air,"
or oxygen

1776 | American Declaration of Independence

1778 | John Singleton Copley paints
Watson and the Shark

Fulhame starts | 1780
experimenting
with metallic cloth

1781 | Cornwallis
surrenders to
Washington at
Yorktown

Husband | 1784
receives MD degree

Birth of | 1787
Louis Daguerre

JOSEPH PRIESTLEY'S
EQUIPMENT FOR
EXPERIMENTS ON
GASES

WATSON AND THE
SHARK

An Essay on Combustion | 1794

Death of Scottish poet Robert Burns | 1796

LORD CHARLES
CORNWALLIS

ROBERT BURNS

1810 | American edition of
An Essay on Combustion

First daguerreotype, an early photograph | 1822

DAGUERREOTYPE
OF LOUIS
DAGUERRE

4 | *The Shimmering Cloth*

Elizabeth Fulhame

Active 1780-1794 | *England*

In 1780 Elizabeth Fulhame, wife of the physician and chemist Thomas Fulhame, came up with the notion of "making cloths of gold, silver, and other metals by chymical processes." Her idea, she thought, would unite art and science by using chemistry to deposit bits of metal in silk, thereby making something new and beautiful. When she described her idea to her husband and a few friends, they told her it probably wouldn't work. She went ahead anyway, beginning a series of experiments that she continued whenever she could gather enough money for supplies.

We have no records of Elizabeth Fulhame's childhood, education, or friendships. She may have been either English or Scottish. Her husband Thomas Fulhame received his MD degree in Edinburgh in 1784 and remained at the university working in chemistry at least until 1790. When the couple married is unknown.

What little we do know about Elizabeth Fulhame comes from the preface to her 1794 book, *An Essay on Combustion, with a View to a New Art of Dy[e]ing and Painting.* The preface, while sparse in biographical details, gives a sense of her lively and determined

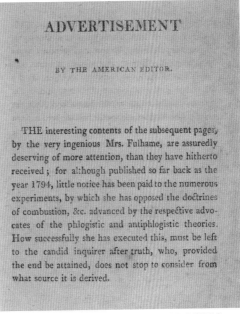

ADVERTISEMENT

BY THE AMERICAN EDITOR.

THE interesting contents of the subsequent pages, by the very ingenious Mrs. Fulhame, are assuredly deserving of more attention, than they have hitherto received; for although published so far back as the year 1794, little notice has been paid to the numerous experiments, by which she has opposed the doctrines of combustion, &c. advanced by the respective advocates of the phlogistic and antiphlogistic theories. How successfully she has executed this, must be left to the candid inquirer after truth, who, provided the end be attained, does not stop to consider from what source it is derived.

PREFACE TO FULHAME'S BOOK ON DYEING

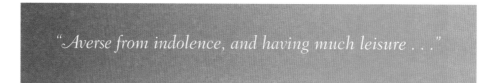

"Averse from indolence, and having much leisure . . ."

personality. "Averse from indolence," she wrote, "and having much leisure, my mind led me to this mode of amusement, which I found entertaining."

Gold and silver, of course, had long been used as ornamentation for clothing, not only as jewelry but also as thin metal sheets wrapped around fibers. What Fulhame proposed to do was something less flashy, less expensive, and more subtle: she would figure out how to use chemistry to bind tiny fragments of pure metal to cloth.

It took Fulhame ten years of careful and often tedious experimentation before she could reliably produce short lengths of metallic cloth. Her equipment was a set of simple glass vessels and cylinders. First she dipped a length of white or colored silk cloth into a solution of metallic salts dissolved in water or ether. Among the metallic ores she used were not only gold and silver but also mercury, tin, lead, platinum, and copper. After soaking, she suspended the cloth in a glass vessel, either dry or still wet, with a cork and a bit of thread. Within the vessel she exposed the cloth to a reducing agent such as hydrogen gas, potassium sulfide, charcoal, or light. Carefully varying the conditions, she took note of changes in color over time, whether the cloth took on a metallic sheen, and whether the reaction appeared to reverse or degrade with exposure to water and air.

By 1790, after ten years of work, Fulhame was proud enough of her creation to show it to friends and men of science, seeking their opinion. She reported quite objectively that some considered it a breakthrough whose "invention would make an era in the arts." Others considered the technique a "pretty conceit" but no more, while others still objected that the cloths were neither rich nor burnished enough in appearance to attract much notice.

A little discouraged, Fulhame kept working to improve her technique, which she even extended to map making, showing how she could deposit gold paint on paper to mark cities and thin lines of silver for rivers. Finally, in 1793, she showed her work to "a celebrated philosopher," most likely the chemist Joseph Priestley, who found her

JOSEPH PRIESTLEY, CHEMIST

work very interesting indeed. Priestley offered to present her investigations to the Royal Society, but in the end, Fulhame decided to publish her own results. Publishing, she decided, would foil "the furacious attempts of the prowling plagiary" and ensure that nobody stole credit for her invention. Moreover, she wrote, even if the craft of dyeing with metals never became the new art she hoped for, her experiments had taught her enough about "combustion"—what we now call oxidation and reduction—that she should share what she had learned.

Like many of the women in this volume and the preceding one, *Magnificent Minds*, Fulhame was well aware that by writing as a woman she risked the patronizing mockery of certain men. Pre-emptively, Fulhame struck first, writing that censure was perhaps inevitable,

> . . . *for some are so ignorant, that they grow sullen and silent, and are chilled with horror at the sight of any thing, that bears the semblance of learning . . . and should the spectre appear in the shape of a* woman, *the pangs which they suffer are truly dismal.*

Fulhame went on to describe with relish the kind of reaction these poor sufferers might display. She anticipated "innuendoes, nods, whispers, sneers, grins, grimace[s], satanic smiles, and witticisms uttered . . . in the nasal obtuse twang, with an affected hauteur . . . shrugs, and a variety of other contortions attending."

Having declawed her potential detractors, Fulhame returned to the matter at hand, describing her experiments. Rather than relate them all in order, she organized her account to illustrate the underlying principles she was investigating. In doing so, she displayed a broad knowledge of controversies and recent findings in the chemical literature.

Fulhame's accounts of her experiments demonstrated careful record keeping. She contrasted experiments that worked with those that did not. Solutions of metal in water, she noted, were successful, while

Phlogiston theory, *first stated in 1667 by Johann Joachim Becher, posited that some materials are rich in a substance called phlogiston that is released through burning. The reason a fire eventually goes out in a closed container, the theory stated, was that the enclosed air had become so full of phlogiston that it could absorb no more. The theory further held that phlogiston is added to metal ore during smelting and lost through processes such as rusting.*

In the 1780s, Antoine Lavoisier challenged phlogiston theory by showing that combustion required a gas, oxygen, that had mass. Addition of oxygen, rather than subtraction of phlogiston, turned out to be the key unifying factor between such processes as burning and rusting.

CHEMISTRY

> *"We are not to be deterred from the investigation*
> *of truth by any authority however great . . ."*

solutions in ether were not. Her overall experience led her to doubt the existence of *phlogiston*, a hypothetical flame-like substance released by combustion. This opinion set her in opposition to chemists like Priestley; on the other hand, she could not quite bring herself to agree with Lavoisier and the anti-phlogiston forces either. Her statement of why she dared to weigh in on the controversy is a ringing defense of the process and ethic of scientific discovery.

> *Finding, the experiments could not be explained on any theory hitherto advanced, I was led to form an opinion different from that of M. Lavoisier, and many great names. Persuaded that we are not to be deterred from the investigation of truth by any authority however great, and that every opinion must stand or fall by its own merits, I venture with diffidence to offer mine to the world, willing to relinquish it, as soon as a more rational appears.*

In fact, what Fulhame described were oxidation-reduction reactions, in which electrons are exchanged between two different substances. Although like other chemists of the time she knew nothing of electrons or even atoms, Fulhame recognized that these two kinds of reactions were reciprocal.

Through her simple series of experiments, Fulhame made a number of important contributions to chemistry. She was the first to show that pure metals can be created by reduction of salts in aqueous (water) solution at room temperature and not only by smelting at high temperature. She also appears to have been the first to describe the role of catalysts, which are elements or compounds that speed a reaction without being consumed by it. Water plays this role in the combustion of carbon, and Fulhame proposed a two-step mechanism by which it did so. She also noted that certain reactions are induced by light.

At first, Fulhame's book appears not to have attracted much attention, although it was immediately translated into German. Gradually her work began to be discussed in chemical treatises.

ANTOINE LAVOISIER, CHEMIST

The physicist and inventor Benjamin Thompson cited "the ingenious and lively Mrs. Fulhame" as an inspiration for his experiments on how light affected chemical reactions. J.F. Coindet, the Swiss physician who first used iodine to treat goiter, cited Fulhame's book for its exploration of the idea of catalysis. On the basis of her experiments with metallic cloth, Fulhame was elected an honorary member of the chemical society of Philadelphia, and in 1810, James Humphreys, an American publisher, re-issued Fulhame's book complete with a laudatory preface.

Recently, historians of photography have noted that Fulhame's methods included a kind of light-based printing with metallic silver similar to the earliest photographic methods. Thus she can be considered a pioneer of the prehistory of photography. Along with her work on fabric dyes, Fulhame's contribution to the birth of photography joined science and art, as she hoped, in a way that still appeals to us today. Through her investigations and careful reasoning, Elizabeth Fulhame helped to create a new branch of the visual arts.

EARLY DAGUERREOTYPE

Photography is the art of capturing an image by allowing light from that image to strike a light-sensitive substance. Around 1800, Thomas Wedgewood tried to capture light from a **camera obscura** *on paper or leather treated with silver nitrate, which darkens when exposed to light. His images were too faint to be useful, however. Nicéphor Niépce used bitumen on pewter to create the first permanent image in 1826, but the process required many hours or even days of exposure.*

In the 1830s, returning to silver salts, Louis Daguerre discovered that after even a short exposure, plates could capture a latent image that could be "developed" by exposure to fumes of mercury, and the first daguerreotypes appeared.

CHEMISTRY

Timeline | 1776-1831

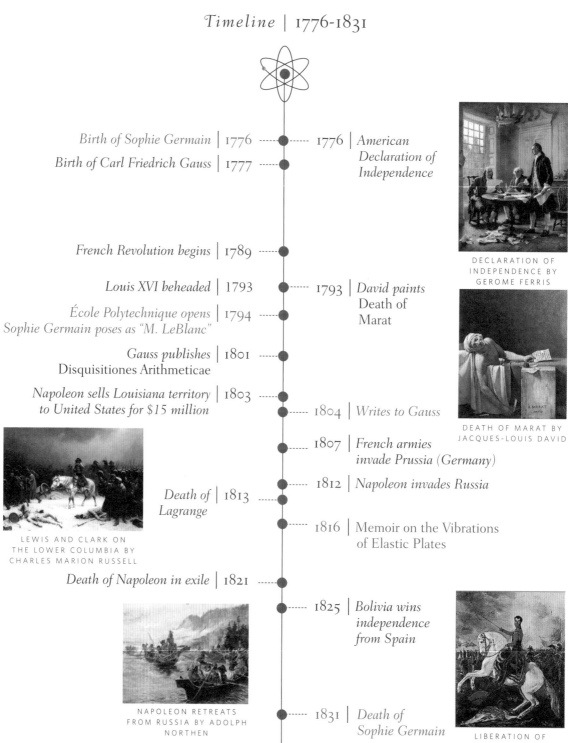

Birth of Sophie Germain | 1776 ------- 1776 | *American Declaration of Independence*

Birth of Carl Friedrich Gauss | 1777 -------

DECLARATION OF INDEPENDENCE BY GEROME FERRIS

French Revolution begins | 1789 -------

Louis XVI beheaded | 1793 ------- 1793 | *David paints Death of Marat*

École Polytechnique opens | 1794 -------
Sophie Germain poses as "M. LeBlanc"

Gauss publishes | 1801 -------
Disquisitiones Arithmeticae

Napoleon sells Louisiana territory | 1803 -------
to United States for $15 million

------- 1804 | *Writes to Gauss*

DEATH OF MARAT BY JACQUES-LOUIS DAVID

------- 1807 | *French armies invade Prussia (Germany)*

------- 1812 | *Napoleon invades Russia*

Death of | 1813 -------
Lagrange

------- 1816 | Memoir on the Vibrations of Elastic Plates

LEWIS AND CLARK ON THE LOWER COLUMBIA BY CHARLES MARION RUSSELL

Death of Napoleon in exile | 1821 -------

------- 1825 | *Bolivia wins independence from Spain*

NAPOLEON RETREATS FROM RUSSIA BY ADOLPH NORTHEN

------- 1831 | *Death of Sophie Germain*

LIBERATION OF BOLIVIA

5 | *Numbers and Vibrating Plates*

Sophie Germain

1776-1831 | *France*

YOUNG SOPHIE GERMAIN

S ophie Germain lived a quiet life in tumul-
tuous times. She grew up in Paris in the
midst of revolution. Her father was a silk
merchant and a deputy to the Estates-
General, representing the Third Estate—all those
who were members of neither the nobility nor the
clergy. Sophie was the second of three daughters.
In 1789, when the Bastille fell and the French
Revolution began, Sophie was only thirteen.
Sheltering from the clamor of the street mobs, she
found a quiet corner in her father's library. There,
in J. F. Montulca's *Histoire des Mathématiques,* she
read about the death of Archimedes: during the
siege of Syracuse, a Roman soldier murdered the
Greek mathematician because he was too deeply
immersed in a geometry problem to respond when
the soldier shouted at him. Sophie decided that a
subject so engrossing must be worth learning, so
she decided to teach herself mathematics.

What more we know about Sophie Germain's
childhood comes from her first biographer, the

Fermat's Last Theorem *intrigued and tormented mathematicians for 358 years. The theorem states that there are no positive integers a, b, and c for which the equation $a^n + b^n = c^n$ is true, if n is greater than two. (If n=2, this is the famous Pythagorean theorem, and a, b, and c do exist). The French mathematician Pierre de Fermat made this conjecture in 1637 and stated that he had thought of a proof, but that the margin of his book was too small to contain it. For centuries afterward, mathematicians worked to prove the conjecture, inventing algebraic number theory along the way. Mathematician Andrew Wiles finally published a proof, which filled hundreds of pages, in 1995.*

Sophie Germain sought to prove the Theorem for the special case where n belongs to a class of prime numbers now known as Germain primes. Prime numbers are whole numbers greater than two that can be divided only by themselves and one. Germain primes are those numbers p for which both p and 2p+1 are prime. Examples of Germain primes include 3, 5, and 11, but not 7, because 2(7) + 1 is equal to 15, which is not a prime number.

mathematician and famous manuscript thief, Guglielmo Libri. Libri corresponded with Germain during her lifetime and wrote about her after her death. Whether he is an entirely reliable witness is uncertain, but his main point appears plausible. Sophie studied too much. Her parents, worried about her health and about the effects of study on the female mind, tried to limit the time she spent working. To get around their restrictions, Sophie took to working in her bedroom at night. When her parents realized what she was doing, they took away her fire, her candles, and even her warmer nightclothes so she would have to keep to her bed and sleep. But Sophie couldn't stay away from her mathematics. She smuggled in more candles, wrapped herself in blankets, and managed to study through the night anyway, even when her ink froze in its pot. Finally her parents gave in, and once convinced he couldn't stop her, her father supported her study of mathematics for the rest of her life.

Germain began her studies with geometry and then taught herself Latin so she could read the books of Newton and Euler. Without a tutor, she plowed through differential calculus. Then, in 1894, Gaspard Monge, a mathematician and Minister of the Marine, established a new school for physical sciences and engineering, the *École Polytechnique*, in Paris. No women were admitted, but by befriending some of the students, Germain managed to collect lecture notes from a course on analysis taught by Joseph Louis Lagrange. Students commonly sent in comments and questions after lectures, so Germain did the same, submitting a composition of her own under the name of a mediocre student who had dropped out, "M. LeBlanc."

So impressed was Lagrange by the sudden improvement and brilliance of M. LeBlanc's work that he sought to meet his gifted student. How surprised he must have been to find she was a twenty-year-old woman! Showing the open-mindedness of a true scientist, he accepted her at once, became her mentor, and introduced her to his circle of mathematical friends.

Still quietly pursuing her studies, Sophie Germain began to correspond with other mathematicians. Among these was Adrien-Marie Legendre, who at the time was focusing on number theory. Through Legendre, Germain learned of Fermat's Last Theorem. Then she read the *Disquisitiones Arithmeticae* of the great German mathematician Carl Friedrich Gauss. Germain worked through the book over a period of three years, trying out proofs of her own. Inspired to take up once more the identity of M. LeBlanc, she wrote to Gauss in 1804 under her pseudonym. She started her letter with an apology: "Unfortunately, the depth of my intellect does not equal the voracity of my appetite, and I feel a kind of temerity in troubling a man of genius…" She presented her attempt at a proof for a special case of

CARL FRIEDRICH GAUSS, BY JENSEN, 1840

Fermat's Last Theorem. Gauss replied kindly, and the two corresponded for many years.

Germain approached Fermat's Last Theorem by trying to prove it for a certain class of prime numbers that have come to be known as Germain primes. Her work was impressive enough that Legendre referred to it in the second edition of his *Essay on Number Theory*, published in 1808. Legendre called Germain's approach "very ingenious."

In 1807, when French armies invaded Prussia, Sophie remembered Archimedes' violent death. Worried for Gauss, she begged the French general, who was a friend of her father's, to ensure his safety. The general visited Gauss, who, it turned out, was fine, but was puzzled as to the identity of "Sophie Germain," who had sent the general to check on him.

Three months later, Germain finally revealed her identity to Gauss, writing to him that "fearing the ridicule attached to a female scientist," she had hidden behind the name of M. LeBlanc. Gauss wrote back in astonishment and delight:

> "... the most noble courage, extraordinary
> talent, and superior genius."

When a woman, because of her sex, our customs and prejudices, encounters infinitely more obstacles than men in familiarizing herself with . . . knotty problems, yet overcomes these fetters and penetrates that which is most hidden, she doubtless has the most noble courage, extraordinary talent, and superior genius.

In a later letter to another friend, Gauss showed that his admiration for Germain's mathematics was genuine. He wrote:

The two test theorems . . . which I also communicated to [LaGrange] some time ago, he considers 'among the most beautiful things and the most difficult to prove.' But Sophie Germain has sent me proofs of these; I have not yet been able to go through them, but I believe they are good.

Despite their friendship, Gauss often did not read all the way through Germain's letters, and he responded only after long intervals. By 1809, Gauss had lost interest in number theory, and he stopped answering Germain's letters.

ERNST FLORENS CHLADNI

About the same time, Sophie Germain turned her attention to a problem where she could apply mathematical theory to a physical observation. In the early 1800s, a German physicist and musician named Ernst Chladni attracted scientific and mathematical attention with a peculiar demonstration. He scattered fine sand or powder across the top of a rigid glass or metal plate mounted on a rod, and then drew a violin bow across the edge of the plate. The plate vibrated, and when it reached a resonant vibration, the sand on top of it arranged itself into patterns. Physicists wondered how the patterns could be explained. What were the underlying laws and equations controlling the vibration of elastic surfaces? Napoleon directed the French Academy of Sciences to offer a prize for the best essay describing these laws and explaining the patterns observed.

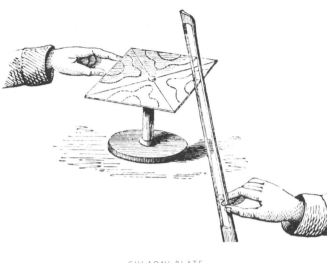

CHLADNI PLATE

Prizes in Napoleonic France

Napoleon, who had started his career as an artillery officer, considered himself a scientist, and as soon as he came to power as First Consul in 1799, he began to patronize the sciences. Wanting the make France the cultural leader of Europe, he established schools, sponsored expeditions, and created a series of prizes, which generally consisted of substantial monetary awards or gold medals.

The Lalande Prize in Astronomy was awarded to a man who discovered a planetoid and to a monk who carefully catalogued the position and movement of 6,000 stars. The Volta Prize in Galvanism and Electricity was awarded three times, once to an Englishman, Sir Humphry Davy. Napoleon also offered single prizes, such as the one for analyzing the Chladni vibrations, won by Sophie Germain, and a prize for food preservation that led Nicolas Appert to perfect a method for heating and bottling food.

Most mathematicians considered the problem too difficult to be worth their time, but Sophie Germain was captivated. She worked on the problem over a number of years, and in 1811, after consulting with Legendre, she submitted a first, anonymous essay to the Academy. The paper was rejected; Lagrange wrote that her method for moving from a line to a two-dimensional surface was inadequate. Undaunted, Germain continued her work and resubmitted in 1813. This time her entry won an honorable mention. That wasn't enough. The problem still intrigued her, and in 1816, she submitted a third entry, this time finally using her own name. This third entry, entitled *Memoir on the Vibrations of Elastic Plates*, finally won the grand prize.

Germain's solution to the problem was a differential equation that was fundamentally correct, although she made some mistakes in setting up the boundary conditions. Her theoretical solution did not quite match the experimental data, and to some mathematicians her explanation revealed the gaps in her formal training. Still, she had clearly taken the problem further than anyone else, and winning a *prix extraordinaire* from the Academy brought her admiring recognition from fellow mathematicians. The mathematician N.H. Navier wrote

MATHEMATICS

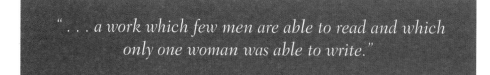

"... a work which few men are able to read and which only one woman was able to write."

of her solution, "It is a work which few men are able to read and which only one woman was able to write." The *Institut de France* celebrated her in a public meeting and allowed her to attend its lectures. The French Academy, however, despite awarding Germain its prize, would not allow her to attend lectures, because she was a woman. Only the wives of male members could attend. Nine years later, the Academy relented and made an exception for Sophie Germain.

In the years following the prize, Germain continued to publish papers on the problem of vibration of elastic surfaces. She also wrote about the philosophy and history of science, although these works were not published until after her death. Number theory, however, remained Sophie Germain's abiding passion. In 1815, the French Academy offered a new prize, this one for a proof of Fermat's Last Theorem. Germain wrote to Gauss that even during the long years of work toward the elasticity prize, she had kept thinking of number theory and longing to return to it. In her letter, Germain described a possible approach toward a general proof of the theorem. Gauss never answered, but Germain proceeded to prove Fermat's Last Theorem for the case of all odd prime numbers less than 100.

STATUE OF SOPHIE GERMAIN

Germain's work in number theory was her greatest contribution to mathematics, but she also continued to work on elastic structures. In 1829, she learned she had breast cancer. She lived two more years, often in pain but always continuing to work on her mathematics. Her last paper on elastic surfaces, which used the idea of mean curvature of a surface, appeared shortly after her death in 1831 at the age of fifty-five.

Sophie Germain, mostly self-taught, made important contributions to both pure and applied mathematics. Her lack of formal mathematics education both helped and hindered her. It gave her the courage to attack problems that others avoided, and it allowed her to come up with novel approaches. At the same time, the fact that other mathematicians treated her with delicacy because she was a woman may have shielded her from the kind of robust debate that could have sharpened her reasoning and improved her work. Nevertheless, her work in elasticity was fundamental in establishing mathematical physics as an area of study, and her work in number theory led to substantial advances. Sophie Germain had a brilliant mathematical mind. Had she had access to the kind of education and mentoring available to men, she might well have achieved even more.

MATHEMATICS

Timeline | 1854-1923

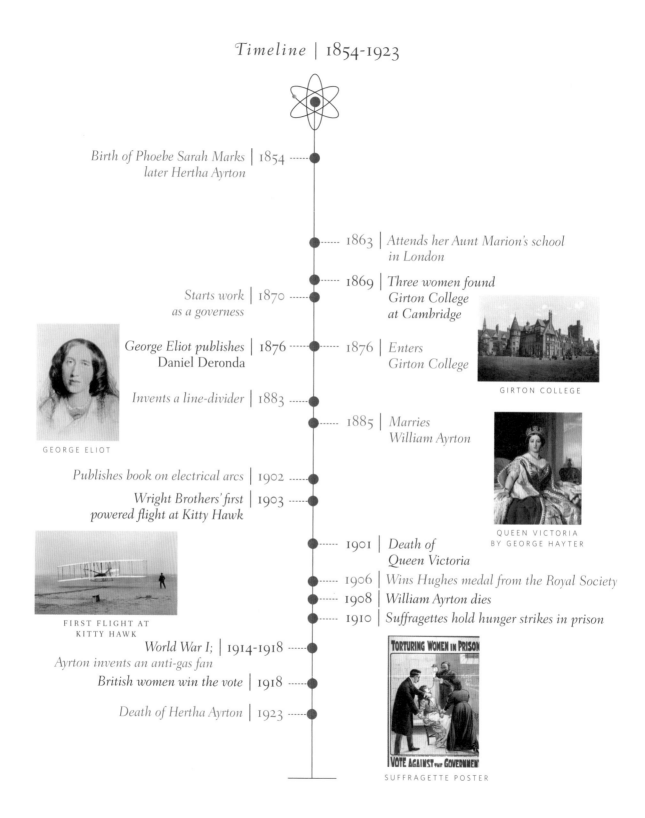

Birth of Phoebe Sarah Marks | 1854
later Hertha Ayrton

1863 | Attends her Aunt Marion's school
in London

1869 | Three women found
Girton College
at Cambridge

Starts work | 1870
as a governess

George Eliot publishes | 1876
Daniel Deronda

1876 | Enters
Girton College

GIRTON COLLEGE

GEORGE ELIOT

Invents a line-divider | 1883

1885 | Marries
William Ayrton

Publishes book on electrical arcs | 1902

Wright Brothers' first | 1903
powered flight at Kitty Hawk

QUEEN VICTORIA
BY GEORGE HAYTER

1901 | Death of
Queen Victoria

1906 | Wins Hughes medal from the Royal Society

1908 | William Ayrton dies

FIRST FLIGHT AT
KITTY HAWK

1910 | Suffragettes hold hunger strikes in prison

World War I; | 1914-1918
Ayrton invents an anti-gas fan

British women win the vote | 1918

Death of Hertha Ayrton | 1923

TORTURING WOMEN IN PRISON

VOTE AGAINST THE GOVERNMENT

SUFFRAGETTE POSTER

6 | *Electrical Suffragette*

Hertha Ayrton

1854-1923 | *England*

HERTHA AYRTON

Phoebe Sarah Marks, who grew up to be Hertha Ayrton, was born in Portsea, England, third of eight children and the first daughter in a family of limited means. Her father, a Jewish refugee from czarist Poland, was a clockmaker and jeweler, but income from his shop was so meager that he took out a license as "a hawker trading on foot." Sarah's mother was the daughter of a glass merchant. When Sarah was seven years old, her father died, and her mother began to work as a seamstress to support her family.

Sarah's maternal aunt, Marion Hartog, managed a school in London, and when Sarah was nine years old, her aunt invited the young girl to come live with her cousins and attend the school. At her Aunt Marion's school Sarah studied French, music, Latin, and mathematics. Her cousins were talented schoolmates; two of the boys became professors and one of the girls became a well-known painter. Sarah struggled at first with discipline and homesickness. She was always untidy, with her hair a mass of unruly dark curls. Once, when unjustly accused of something she didn't do, she went on a hunger strike for two and a half days before the adults gave in. Sarah immersed herself in enthusiasms for drawing and theatricals, and she excelled at her studies, particularly in mathematics. In time she grew so confident of her own knowledge that her cousins teased her:

> *Sarah, with voice so clear and low,*
> *So sure of all she doesn't know!*

Having completed school at the age of sixteen, and determined to help support her brothers and invalid sister, Sarah Marks sought work as governess to a London family. Once she had worked long enough to obtain a good reference, she left the post to take on daily pupils instead, most often coaching them in mathematics.

As she became financially independent, Sarah began to question her Jewish religion, and soon she was calling herself a freethinker. Her circle of friends widened to include Ottilie Blind, daughter of a well-off German Jewish immigrant. Ottilie liked to call Sarah "Hertha" after the title character in A.C. Swinburne's "mystic atheistic democratic anthropological poem," where Hertha is a mother-goddess opposed to patriarchal religion. Soon, Sarah Marks began to call herself Hertha, and most people she met later never knew her by any other name.

Ottilie encouraged Hertha in her dream of furthering her education. Together in Ottilie's rooms, after a full day of teaching, the two girls had high tea and studied for the new Cambridge University Examination for Women. Hertha passed the exam with honors in English and mathematics in 1874. Ottilie also introduced her friend to a set of accomplished feminist women, one of whom, Barbara Bodichon, proved vital to Hertha's future. Bodichon, a wealthy and well-known painter, had

BARBARA BODICHON

just helped to establish a new women's college at Cambridge. Impressed by Hertha's eagerness and vitality, Bodichon offered her a scholarship to study at the new Girton College.

Grateful and excited as she was, Hertha could not accept right away. She still needed to help support her family, and at one point she brought her invalid sister Winnie to London to live with her. Winnie's needs meant that Hertha could no longer go out to teach in the afternoons, so instead, like her mother, she turned to embroidery and needlework to support the household. Among her customers was the author George Eliot, for whom she embroidered a fine bonnet. The two had become friends through Mme. Bodichon, and it is likely that the character of the Jewish girl Mariah in Eliot's novel *Daniel Deronda* is based partly on Hertha Marks.

Eventually one of Hertha's brothers contributed to help send Winnie to school, and in 1876, at the age of 22, Hertha Marks finally had her chance to attend college. At Girton she sang in the chorus and organized a volunteer fire brigade. During holidays she stayed at Barbara Bodichon's country estate, working for her benefactress in partial repayment for her scholarship. She studied Greek and literature and most of all, mathematics. Her tutors and classmates noted her tendency to rush into applications before she completely mastered a mathematical theory. When, after three years of study, she took Cambridge's feared Tripos examination in mathematics, she was disappointed to receive only a third class score.

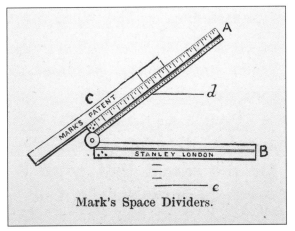

Mark's Space Dividers.

LINE DIVIDER PATENTED BY HERTHA MARKS,
COURTESY OF RKS

After college, Hertha rented a flat with a college classmate and continued to teach and coach students in mathematics. Her income rose to 250 pounds sterling, which allowed her to begin paying back college loans. And she kept thinking about applications. In 1883 she became intrigued with the problem of how to divide a line segment into any number of equal parts. She created a device to do this—a line-divider—and perfected it over the course of a year. With Bodichon's help, Hertha patented the invention, and she delivered an invited paper on its use to the Physical Society. Editorial writers in both England and France cited the new line-divider as justification for the higher education of women. The *Revue Scientifique* remarked, "It is often claimed that women are capable only of assimilation and not of invention; the device which we have just described is a *mathematical* proof to the contrary."

The success of her first invention stoked Hertha's interest and confidence in applied science, and she decided to learn more about electricity. She arranged to attend Finsbury Technical College four nights a week to study electricity with Professor William Ayrton. Ayrton was a widower, clever, courtly, and a bit unworldly. He had worked in India and Japan. A true feminist, he had encouraged his first wife to study medicine; now he encouraged Hertha Marks in her scientific ambition. In 1885, Hertha married him, after writing a long letter to her mother explaining why he was an ideal partner despite not being Jewish.

With marriage, Hertha Ayrton found herself once again balancing family responsibilities and scientific interests. William Ayrton's daughter Edith came home from school to live with the couple. Soon she was joined by a new sister, Barbara Bodichon Ayrton. Hertha was often ill in the early years of her marriage, but in 1888 she rallied to deliver a series of six elementary lectures for women on electricity and how it might eventually save labor in the home. Electricity could drive

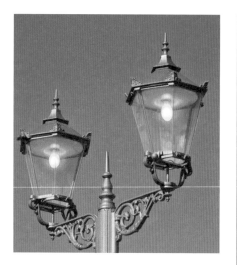

Street Lighting. *City dwellers have never liked walking home in the dark. In urban Greece and Rome, lamps that burned vegetable oil provided some light. Roman slaves called* lanternarii *hung oil lamps outside the house or carried them through the streets to light their masters' way.*

By the 1500s, the main streets of London and Paris were illuminated. Laws required city residents to hang lanterns by their doorways and to keep lamps burning in windows that faced the street.

The earliest gas lamps, developed in the 1800s, used piped coal gas. Oil gas and kerosene came later. In 1875, the first electrical or arc lamps, called Yablochov candles after their inventor, provided a harsh, bright light. Gradually these arc lamps were replaced by incandescent lighting and then by today's high intensity halide, or more recently, LED lamps.

a sewing machine, she told them. It could wind clocks, clean silver, and even magnify sound.

When Barbara Bodichon died in 1891, she left Hertha an independent income that allowed her to support her mother and hire a housekeeper to help run the household. Newly liberated, Hertha created a laboratory on the top floor of her house and pursued her own investigations in electricity. Her experiments took on fresh importance when Professor Ayrton was invited to present a paper in Chicago. In his absence, Hertha enlisted his students in a rushed program of experiments, updating him on the results in regular letters.

> *"It is immensely more interesting to plunge straight into a thing . . ."*

Emboldened by her success with these experiments, Hertha Ayrton embarked on a series of investigations on electrical arcs, the bright carbon lights that were replacing gas lamps in streets and theaters. Instead of fretting about her weak theoretical grounding in physics, Ayrton wrote, "Getting into something fresh without preconceived ideas, one sometimes sees things in a light that might escape those better grounded in the subject. It is immensely more interesting to plunge straight into a thing like this than to begin with the alphabet of it!"

For her experiments, she designed equipment that her husband then had his students and assistants at the Technical College manufacture for her. She began her investigations by asking why electrical arcs hissed. Carbon arc lights consist of two carbon electrodes separated by a short distance. A column of ionized carbon vapor between the two electrodes allows a continuous spark, like lightning, to cross the gap. Silent and bright when they are first lit, arc lamps soon begin to hum, hiss, and flicker with a weaker green and purple light. Through a series of careful experiments, Ayrton was able to show that the hissing was caused by oxygen coming in contact with the electrodes.

Ayrton's findings attracted broad interest. She delivered a paper to the Institution of Electrical Engineers, or IEE, for which she was awarded a prize of ten pounds sterling. She published in *Nature* and wrote a series of articles for *The Electrician*. In 1899, the IEE elected her a full member, making her the first woman to be so honored. Hertha lectured in fluent French at the International Electrical Congress in Paris. She demonstrated her apparatus and her findings at a *conversazione*, or public science day, of the Royal Society, and she chaired the section on physical sciences for the International Congress of Women in London in July 1899. Speaking to women who might become scientists, Ayrton urged them to do their own experiments before turning to books for explanations—that way the explanations would make more sense.

Hertha Ayrton always preferred doing experiments to writing them up, but in 1902 she finally finished a book on her experiments with electrical arcs. The book immediately became

AYRTON IN HER HOME LABORATORY,
COURTESY OF RONALD SMELTZER

the recognized textbook on the subject. Meanwhile, a Professor Perry read one of her papers before the Royal Society to a good reception, and colleagues put her name forward for membership in the Society. After consulting their legal counsel, the officers decided that as a married woman, who had no legal standing under English common law, Hertha Ayrton was not eligible for membership.

Professor William Ayrton's health had been fragile for some time, and when his doctors prescribed a rest cure by the seaside, the couple left their experimental apparatus behind. Walking the beaches, Hertha Ayrton became interested in the motion of the waves and their effects on ripples in the sand. She noted that ripples did not form, as one might expect, on the front where the waves pounded into the sand. Rather, they appeared under water, beneath a stationary wave as it rose and fell. Soon she was testing her observations in bathtubs, basins, and specially constructed wave tanks.

Soon Hertha Ayrton was lecturing again. When she read a paper on "The Origin and Growth of Ripplemark" before the Royal Society in June 1904, it was the first paper delivered to that august body by a woman. She accompanied her talk with demonstrations using sand and water in glass tanks. As before, she followed her formal lectures with popular ones for women and others. Using ground black pepper scattered in the water, she demonstrated that a rising wave creates vortices around any irregularity in the sand floor, and that once one ripple is created in the sand beneath oscillating waves, ripples form in pairs on either side of it at regular intervals. In response to criticisms and questions raised about her explanations of these findings, she invented a small pressure gauge, which she patented in 1915.

Both Professor Ayrton and his wife emphasized that her scientific investigations were separate and independent from his. She later wrote, "My husband foresaw that if we collaborated any merit that might attach to our work would be attributed to him . . . and he therefore, out of a chivalrous regard for my scientific reputation, refused ever to collaborate with me." She had noticed that when Pierre Curie died in 1906, English newspapers eulogized him as the discoverer of radium. Acidly, Hertha reminded readers that it was Pierre's wife Marie who made that discovery. She wrote to the Westminster *Gazette*, "Errors are notoriously hard to kill, but an error that ascribes to a man what was actually the work of a woman has more lives than a cat."

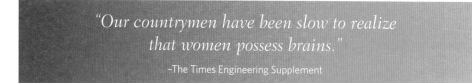

"*Our countrymen have been slow to realize that women possess brains.*"
–The Times Engineering Supplement

In 1906 Hertha Ayrton received the Royal Society's Hughes medal—the first time it was awarded to a woman alone—for her "experimental investigations on the electric arc, and also upon sand ripples." As when she invented the line-divider, some in the press seized on her accomplishment to make a general statement about the capacity of women. The *Times Engineering Supplement* opined, "Our countrymen have been slow to realize that women possess brains; we are too apt to regard them as the mere helpmeets of men . . . It seems that the time has now come when woman should be permitted to take her place in the ranks of all our learned bodies."

Ayrton deplored the fact that two learned bodies in England, Oxford and Cambridge Universities, still did not admit women. To those who pointed out the progress women had already made, she answered, "Why do I dwell on the churlishness of two universities when all the others are open to us? Perhaps because a toothache is sufficient to make us forget that all the rest of our body is free from pain."

The capacity of women, and especially their fitness for the vote, had become an urgent question in early twentieth century Britain. Hertha Ayrton had always been a feminist, and as women became more militant in their demand for the vote, she supported their movement with donations and hospitality. She preferred to avoid public speaking, which she hated, instead trying to make her case for women by continuing her scientific work. Once, when asked to give a speech, she wrote, "I suppose I ought to do it, but oh, dear me! I wish the Bill would pass so that I could be left in peace to do my own work . . . I feel a sort of inward white rage that we should have to waste our lives and our energies as we are doing, in order to secure the most elementary justice." When she did speak, she demanded greater rights for women but also urged women to take advantage of the opportunities open to them and to enter the professions if they could.

> *"I wish the Bill would pass so that I could be left in peace to do my own work."*

From 1906 on, Ayrton was increasingly occupied by caring for her ailing husband. His failing health led her to break their rule against collaboration. The navy had asked William Ayrton to create new specifications for carbon arc searchlights, and Hertha was well qualified to take on some of his burden. Together the Ayrtons wrote three treatises on the topic. Then, in 1908, William Ayrton died, and his grief-stricken wife wrote the fourth and final report alone.

As the fight for the vote continued, both Hertha Ayrton and her daughter Barbara became members of the Women's Social and Political Union (WSPU). On Black Friday, November 18, 1910, Ayrton was one of 300 women who marched on Parliament, where they were manhandled by police and roving gang members. Women's civil disobedience continued, and a number of suffragettes were arrested. In prison they launched hunger strikes, and the government, weary of trying to force-feed them, hit on a new strategy. Women prostrated by hunger were released to their friends for care and feeding; then, when they recovered, the government re-arrested them. Hertha Ayrton's house became one of the prime sanctuaries for women released from prison. Eventually she nurtured forty of them back to health, even as detectives watched the house night and day, intent on ensuring that the miscreant women did not slip away.

In 1912, Ayrton also sheltered Marie Curie and her two daughters, who fled the withering attention of the French press following the revelation of Marie's affair with Paul Langevin. Ayrton's feminism appears to have left more of an imprint on Marie's two daughters, Irène and Eve, than it did on Marie herself.

On one occasion in 1912, as several women including Hertha's daughter Barbara were arrested, rumors swirled that the government was about to raid the WSPU offices and confiscate all their funds. A suffragette brought a check to Hertha Ayrton; she deposited it in her bank, then withdrew it and transferred the money abroad, along with a check of her own for a thousand pounds sterling.

POSTER SHOWING FORCE FEEDING OF A SUFFRAGETTE

GAS WARFARE ON THE EASTERN FRONT,
BUNDESARCHIV

Poison Gas in World War I. *The French were the first to use a kind of tear gas against German attackers in Belgium. The Germans soon responded with the far more deadly chlorine gas. When a green cloud of chlorine gas released from cylinders in the German lines drifted across the French lines, soldiers began to choke. They died of suffocation as the gas reacted with moisture in their lungs to form hydrochloric acid. When the British began using chlorine gas too, the Germans responded with the far more deadly phosgene gas, which caused symptoms only after a latent period of hours or days.*

By 1917, most Western soldiers had effective gas masks, but mustard gas, developed next, soaked into soldiers' woolen uniforms and caused severe blistering all over the body. If it reached the eyes, it caused blindness, usually temporary. By that time, armies were shooting gas canisters to enemy lines in exploding shells. Still, if the wind changed, the gas sometimes drifted back over the lines of the sending army. The major purpose of gas attacks was to spread terror among enemy troops. Many army leaders felt, as one British general expressed it, that gas attacks were "a cowardly form of warfare" as well as one that offered neither side a clear advantage. After the war, the Geneva Protocol of 1925 outlawed the use of poison gas.

Then World War I arrived, sweeping away both the campaign for suffrage and ordinary scientific work. Ayrton helped fund one of Marie Curie's traveling X-ray vans. Then, hearing of the devastating effects of poison gas on British soldiers, she turned her mind to what she had learned about air as a fluid. It might be possible, she thought, for men in the trenches to wave the gas away with hand fans. At once she went to work in her laboratory, building and testing models. She burned paper for smoke, designed tall, squarish fans, and came up with what she thought was an effective technique for waving the smoke or gas away. Then she lobbied the War Department to give her invention a chance. Bureaucratic response was slow, but finally the fans underwent tests in France. There the trials suggested that the fan worked for gas floating at less than nine miles per hour.

CLEARING A TRENCH OF GAS WITH AYRTON FANS

Early in the war, that might have helped, but now most poison gas was being delivered in explosive shells. On the other hand, the testers reported, the fans were surprisingly effective for clearing gas out of a trench once it had settled in.

Still, adoption of the invention was slow, and at times Ayrton lost her optimism. "After all, the poor soldiers are little better off for all my work," she wrote, but she kept working to improve her design. By the end of the war, more than 100,000 Ayrton fans had been deployed in France, usually with no training in their use and often spaced at intervals too far apart to be effective. Some soldiers said mockingly that the fans made good firewood, but others swore by them. One soldier who wrote for *Punch* after the war assured Ayrton in a letter, "Anyhow, there are thousands and thousands of inarticulate soldier persons who are extremely grateful to you."

At the end of the war, Parliament recognized at last that it could no longer withhold the vote from the women who had so gallantly rallied to defend the country. In 1918 the Representation of the People Act extended the franchise to all women over the age of thirty.

In 1919, Ayrton presented her paper to the Royal Society on how the anti-gas fan created vortices. She continued to work on ripples and vortices until her death in 1923 at the age of sixty-nine. Friends remembered her courage, her generosity, and the grace with which she combined her personal and professional lives.

DUSTCOVER OF *THE CALL*,
BY EDITH AYRTON ZANGWILL

The year after Hertha Ayrton's death, her stepdaughter, Edith Ayrton Zangwill, published a novel called *The Call* that makes thinly veiled references to her stepmother. The novel's heroine, Ursula Hibbert, is a chemist, working in a home laboratory, who suffers gender discrimination. After initial reluctance, she becomes a militant feminist. During World War I, she invents a device to extinguish chemical fires on the battlefield, but the War Office rejects her invention as useless. As a result of War Office intransigence, Ursula's fiancé is severely injured on the battlefield. The book reflects the opinion of many feminists of the time that Ayrton's fans were never given a fair chance to demonstrate their usefulness. The scientific community did not agree. Although Ayrton presented several well-received technical papers on the project, most scientists remained skeptical of her anti-gas fans.

Hertha Ayrton was the first woman electrical engineer, and her example and activism helped to open doors for the women who followed. She asked no more than that women be given access to the same opportunities as men, writing, "The idea of 'women and science' is entirely irrelevant. Either a woman is a good scientist, or she is not; in any case she should be given opportunities, and her work should be studied from the scientific, not the sex, point of view."

Timeline | 1871-1953

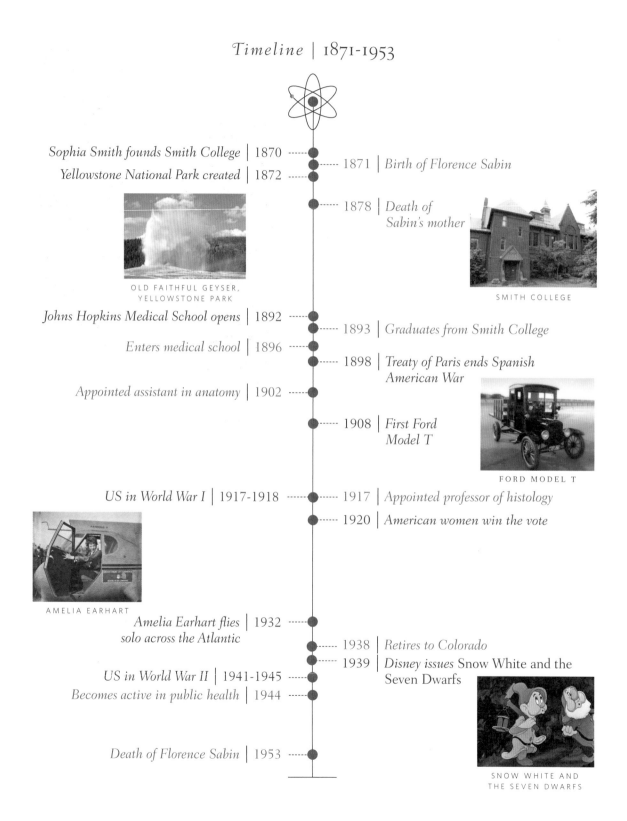

Sophia Smith founds Smith College | 1870

1871 | *Birth of Florence Sabin*

Yellowstone National Park created | 1872

1878 | *Death of Sabin's mother*

OLD FAITHFUL GEYSER, YELLOWSTONE PARK

SMITH COLLEGE

Johns Hopkins Medical School opens | 1892

1893 | *Graduates from Smith College*

Enters medical school | 1896

1898 | *Treaty of Paris ends Spanish American War*

Appointed assistant in anatomy | 1902

1908 | *First Ford Model T*

FORD MODEL T

US in World War I | 1917-1918 ----- 1917 | *Appointed professor of histology*

1920 | *American women win the vote*

AMELIA EARHART

Amelia Earhart flies | 1932
solo across the Atlantic

1938 | *Retires to Colorado*

1939 | *Disney issues* Snow White and the Seven Dwarfs

US in World War II | 1941-1945

Becomes active in public health | 1944

Death of Florence Sabin | 1953

SNOW WHITE AND THE SEVEN DWARFS

7 | *Anatomical Researcher*

Florence Rena Sabin

1871-1953 | *United States*

Florence Sabin, who became the leading female medical researcher of her generation, benefited from the foresight and generosity of a pair of determined women. After the Civil War, women in America began to use their own money to support the education of their sisters. In 1870, Sophia Smith, the last remaining child of a wealthy farmer, left $387,468 in her will to found a women's college in Northampton, Massachusetts. Her aim, she wrote, was "to furnish for my own sex means and facilities for education equal to those that are afforded now in our Colleges to young men." Smith College, the first women's college founded by a woman, opened its doors to fourteen students the following year.

Four years later, the Johns Hopkins University opened in Baltimore, Maryland as a college for men only. Over the next fifteen years, the university worked on plans for a

SABIN'S BIRTHPLACE, NATIONAL LIBRARY OF MEDICINE

medical school. In most medical schools at the time, poorly prepared students hurried through a superficial curriculum. The Hopkins founders envisioned a more rigorous education delivered by an illustrious faculty. Unfortunately, though they had hoped to open the medical school in 1889, the university trustees found themselves short of funds and had to delay. At that point, a wealthy spinster, Mary Elizabeth Garrett, came forward with an offer. She would raise a Women's Fund of $100,000 if the new medical school would admit women on an equal basis with men. The trustees responded that they needed $500,000 to start the school. Eventually, Garrett increased her personal contribution to $354,764.50, equivalent to over $6.5 million today. With the admission of its first class in 1892, Johns Hopkins became the first co-educational medical school in America. (Harvard Medical School, by contrast, did not admit women until 1945.)

YOUNG SABIN, NATIONAL LIBRARY OF MEDICINE

Florence Sabin was born in 1871 in Central City, Colorado. Her mother Serena was a schoolteacher who moved to Colorado from the Confederacy during the Civil War. Her father George was a mining engineer whose Huguenot ancestors had fled from Europe to America in the seventeenth century. When Florence was seven years old, her mother died from puerperal fever, an infection following childbirth. Florence and her older sister Mary lived in Denver, then with an uncle in Chicago, and finally with their paternal grandparents in Vermont. Both attended Vermont Academy in Saxtons River, where their teachers encouraged them to go on to college. Although Florence did well in math and science, what she really wanted was to become a pianist. One day a classmate bluntly told her that her musical talent was only average. Though she must have been disappointed, Florence quickly pulled herself together and applied to Smith College, where she majored in zoology, the study of animal life.

At Smith, the college physician encouraged her to explore the new opportunities available to women for medical study at Johns Hopkins. Intrigued but unable to afford the tuition, Florence worked for three years as a high school teacher and saved her money. In 1896 she moved to Baltimore and entered medical school as one of fourteen women in a class of forty-five.

During medical school, Florence Sabin found herself attracted to research. Her skills in the laboratory earned her a place working with the anatomist Franklin Mall. Mall was a German-trained anatomist dedicated to the idea of bringing scientific research to American medical education. He taught not by lecture, but by working beside his students. One of his assistants wrote of Mall's "earnest and sincere desire to make the neophyte an independent worker." Students of the liberal arts, used to polished lectures and carefully constructed laboratory experiences, often felt that he wasn't giving them enough direction. Sabin found the opposite, and rose to the challenges Mall

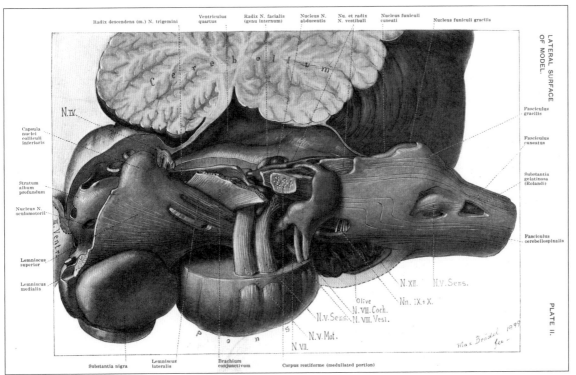

gave her. Mall became her mentor and role model, someone so important to her that she later wrote his biography. While still a student, she published a paper on the detailed anatomy of the VIIIth cranial nerve, which carries signals for both hearing and balance. Then, on Mall's advice, she took on a project describing the three-dimensional anatomy of a newborn baby's brain. She focused on the three "lower" sections of the brain, the medulla, midbrain, and pons. Sabin's thorough study of the topic eventually became a book, published in 1901 and widely used as a textbook.

Sabin graduated from medical school in 1900, and along with another top student, also a woman, won a prestigious Johns Hopkins internship under the famous physician Sir William Osler. The internship year only confirmed her conviction that what she really wanted to do was research. Mary Garrett's fund came through again, this time with a research fellowship in the Anatomy Department and a stipend of $800. Once more, Franklin Mall, the department's chair, became her mentor. With one book already published, Sabin continued her studies in neuroanatomy, impressing her superiors well enough that in 1902 she was appointed assistant in anatomy, becoming the first woman faculty member in the medical school.

Along with anatomy, Sabin taught medical students embryology, covering how fetal organs develop from conception to birth. In her research, Sabin focused on how embryos develop their vascular system, including arteries, veins, and capillaries, and their lymphatic system, whose thin-walled vessels drains waste fluids from tissue. By injecting colored fluid into the lymphatic vessels,

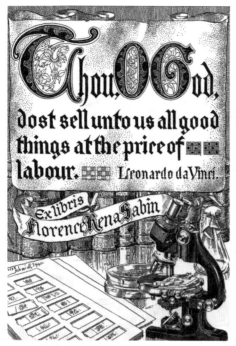

SABIN'S PERSONAL BOOK PLATE

she determined that lymphatic vessels grow from veins. Her work was important enough that in 1917 she was appointed professor of histology, or the microscopic study of tissues, becoming the first woman full professor in the medical school.

Although she never married, Sabin was sociable and fond of entertaining. In their biographical memoir, Philip McMaster and Michael Heidelberger wrote that she loved to invite students to dinner:

. . . she showed a phenomenal flair for social entertainment in her home, a love for and skill at the art of cookery . . . carried on at times with fun and a pleasant burlesque of the exactness of scientific techniques . . . stop watch turning steaks at exactly every third minute, on the dot of the 180th second; of scalding the dishes afterwards and cleaning them as though they were to be used for the next experiment in the laboratory.

"Of course I'll stay. I have research in progress."

Despite Sabin's prominence and popularity, her colleagues sometimes still resisted female leadership in medicine. In 1919, when the chairmanship of the Anatomy Department fell open, the faculty passed over Sabin, a full professor, in favor of a male candidate who was only an associate professor, one rank lower. Sabin's students, offended on her behalf, drew up a petition to reverse the decision. Mary Garrett's Women's Fund committee registered their outrage. One of them asked Sabin if she intended to remain at Hopkins after this slight. Sabin answered, "Of course I'll stay. I have research in progress."

Research came first, and at that time, Sabin was deeply immersed in her study of the origins and early development of blood vessels, connective tissue such as cartilage, and blood cells. She was perfecting the technique of supravital staining, which involves staining cells and observing them while they are still living. Although most of her studies were aimed at basic understanding, she also did research that related directly to patient care. For example, in 1920, she studied end-to-end intestinal anastomosis (an-AS-toe-MOE-siss) , an operation pioneered by Dr. William Halstead in which he surgically cut out a section of diseased intestine and then sewed the two loose ends back together. Sabin investigated how cells repaired the gap, research which led to better surgical techniques for closing the intestinal wound. As a result of both her basic and her applied research, Sabin was elected president of the American Association of Anatomists in 1924. The following year she became the first woman elected to the National Academy of Sciences.

Since 1923, Simon Flexner, director of the Rockefeller Institute for Medical Research, had been recruiting Sabin to join the Institute as head of its Department of Cellular Studies. Although she enjoyed teaching and the interaction with students that Hopkins provided, Sabin eventually decided that she would enjoy having fewer distractions and the chance to devote herself fully to research. In 1925, she joined the Rockefeller Institute as the first woman to become a full member.

SABIN AT JOHNS HOPKINS

During his life, "robber baron" John D. Rockefeller, the founder of Standard Oil, was the world's richest man and its most generous philanthropist. He established missions and funded higher education with major donations to Spelman College, the University of Chicago, and Denison University. In 1901, influenced by William Osler, he established the **Rockefeller Institute for Medical Research**, *the country's first institution dedicated entirely to medical research. A hospital devoted to clinical research followed. Twenty-four Rockefeller scientists have won Nobel Prizes and twenty-one have received the National Medal of Science.*

In 1965, in keeping with its increasing role in graduate education, the Institute was renamed the Rockefeller University. It continues to prepare young scientists from around the world to become leaders of biomedical research.

At the Rockefeller Institute, Sabin turned her attention to the pathology of tuberculosis, using her techniques of cell staining to closely examine how cells respond to chemical signals from the tubercle bacillus, the germ causing tuberculosis. She was able

SABIN WITH COLORADO GOVERNOR KNOUS
AFTER HE SIGNED THE SABIN LAWS

to demonstrate the role of white blood cells, especially monocytes, in defending the body against tuberculosis and other infections. During this period she also wrote the biography of her mentor in anatomy, Franklin Mall. In her introduction, she wrote of Mall, "His original and memorable personality lives in the minds of his colleagues, his pupils, and his friends far more vividly than in the pages of this book . . . [The writer's] start in research as a medical student and her opportunity for a career in scientific medicine she owes wholly to him."

By this time, Florence Sabin was recognized as the most prominent woman scientist of her generation. In 1931, a poll by *Good Housekeeping* magazine named her one of the twelve most eminent living American women.

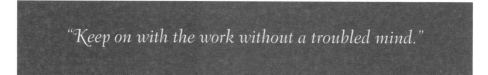

"Keep on with the work without a troubled mind."

In 1936, the young medical researcher Helen Taussig wrote to Sabin for career advice. Should she, Taussig, remain at Johns Hopkins, where she earned less than her male peers and where male faculty members still seemed opposed to women's advancement? Taussig wrote that while money was not a deciding factor for her, "my self-respect demands that the institution I work in, should have confidence in me." Sabin advised her to stay on "and keep on with the work without a troubled mind." Research came first.

In 1938, Florence Sabin retired from the Rockefeller Institute and returned to Colorado to live with her sister. She had published over a hundred scientific papers during her career, and after retirement she continued to attend research conferences, correspond with colleagues, and sit on advisory committees for foundations.

Then, in 1944, Sabin was asked to chair the health sub-committee of Colorado's committee for post-war planning. Sabin created a second career for herself as a strong advocate for public health. Her committee advocated for a series of laws that became known as the "Sabin program." Four of her six bills became law in 1947. Next, she was appointed chair of the Interim Board of Health and Hospitals in Denver, and then Manager of the Denver Department of Health and Charities. She worked to improve city sanitation and increased the enforcement of health regulations for restaurants and food suppliers. She also ramped up screening of the population for syphilis and tuberculosis. Under her leadership, the number of citizens infected by tuberculosis fell by half over two years, and the rate of syphilis infection fell by over ninety percent.

Sabin received many awards and honors for her work both in basic science and in public health, including the American Women's Association medal for eminent achievement in 1941 and the Albert Lasker Award for Public Service in 1951. Sabin died in Denver, Colorado, in 1953. In 1959, the state of Colorado placed a statue of Florence Rena Sabin in the statuary hall of the U.S. Capitol, and in the 2000s, Johns Hopkins School of Medicine named two of its four student "houses" or divisions after Helen Taussig and Florence Sabin, two of its pioneering and prominent graduates and faculty members in medicine.

FRANKLIN MALL

Tuberculosis, *often called TB, has been around for millennia. It has been found in the bones of prehistoric people from 4000 BC and in Egyptian mummies. Hippocrates called it phthisis and described feverish patients who coughed up blood and almost always died of the disease. In later centuries, Europeans called TB "consumption" because of the way its victims wasted away.*

In 1882, Robert Koch identified the tuberculosis bacillus, Mycobacterium tuberculosis, and proved that it caused the disease. The only treatment at the time was isolation in a sanatorium, where wealthy patients enjoyed fresh air and good food, while poor patients were set to work. In some cases doctors surgically collapsed an infected lung to "rest" it. This could be curative because it deprived the TB bacillus of the oxygen it needed to grow. Still, fifty percent of patients died within five years.

In 1946, the discovery of streptomycin offered the first cure for tuberculosis. However, the bacillus rapidly develops drug resistance and often causes disease beyond the lungs—in the bones, kidneys, lymph nodes and beyond. Today, tuberculosis newly infects about one percent of the world population each year. Many cases remain latent, but those that become active require treatment with multiple drugs for many months.

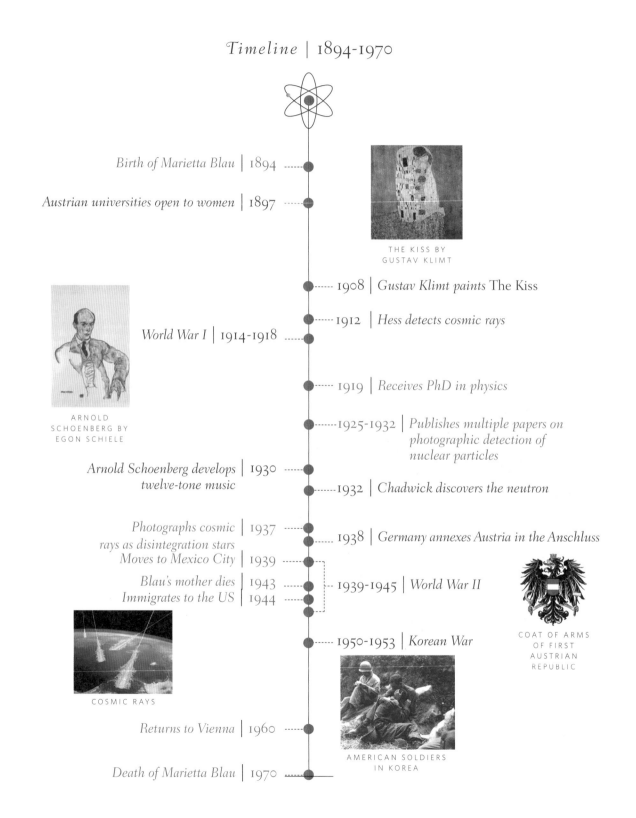

Timeline | 1894-1970

Birth of Marietta Blau | 1894

Austrian universities open to women | 1897

THE KISS BY
GUSTAV KLIMT

1908 | Gustav Klimt paints The Kiss

1912 | Hess detects cosmic rays

World War I | 1914-1918

1919 | Receives PhD in physics

1925-1932 | Publishes multiple papers on
photographic detection of
nuclear particles

ARNOLD
SCHOENBERG BY
EGON SCHIELE

Arnold Schoenberg develops | 1930
twelve-tone music

1932 | Chadwick discovers the neutron

Photographs cosmic | 1937
rays as disintegration stars

1938 | Germany annexes Austria in the Anschluss

Moves to Mexico City | 1939

Blau's mother dies | 1943

1939-1945 | World War II

Immigrates to the US | 1944

COAT OF ARMS
OF FIRST
AUSTRIAN
REPUBLIC

1950-1953 | Korean War

COSMIC RAYS

Returns to Vienna | 1960

AMERICAN SOLDIERS
IN KOREA

Death of Marietta Blau | 1970

[66]

8 | *Starburst Traces of Cosmic Rays*

Marietta Blau

1894-1970 | *Austria*

arietta Blau was a shy, quiet woman whose important contributions to particle physics were interrupted when the Nazi party rose to power in Europe. Like Lise Meitner and Emmy Noether, both profiled in *Magnificent Minds,* she felt compelled to flee her home at the height of her scientific powers. While her former student, a Nazi party member, carried on and took credit for their work, Blau struggled in a series of unrewarding jobs in exile. Although after World War II she had an opportunity to work as a researcher again, and even to return to Vienna, her scientific career never fully recovered, and when she died, no one wrote her scientific obituary. Yet she was nominated for the Nobel Prize three times, and her work in capturing photographic traces of cosmic rays and particle interactions undergirded the Nobel Prize work of other particle physicists.

Marietta Blau was born in Vienna on April 29, 1894 to an upper-middle-class Jewish family. It was the year the last czar took power in Europe and three years before the first women in Austria were allowed a university education. The family lived in an elegant part of Vienna only a few blocks from Lise Meitner's home. Marietta's father, Markus Blau, was a successful

MARIETTA BLAU

lawyer who composed music in his spare time, and her brother Otto later directed a music publishing company. When Marietta was only a year old and Otto was two, the death of their older brother Fritz devastated their mother, Florentine. A year later, another boy, Ludwig, was born.

Marietta attended an elementary school staffed by students and faculty of a teacher training college. Once she surprised her teachers by bringing several mice to school with her, but in general she was an excellent and obedient pupil. When she was eleven, she began attending a private upper school for girls, the first school in Austria that prepared girls for the *Matura,* or general university entrance exam. One year, perhaps because of poor health, Marietta studied at home instead of attending school, but soon she returned. She chose German, Greek, civics, and mathematics as her *Matura* subjects, and she passed with distinction.

In the winter semester of 1914/1915, Marietta Blau entered the University of Vienna, having chosen mathematics and physics as her subjects of study. World War I had just begun, and the proportion of women in the universities rose sharply as young men went to war. Blau's two brothers both fought and survived the war, but her cousin Franz was killed in action.

In 1916, Blau contracted tuberculosis and had to temporarily leave the university for a sanatorium, a specialized hospital where, in the absence of antibiotics, the treatment consisted of fresh air, good food, and rest. Blau recovered well enough to continue her studies, including a year-long laboratory course at the privately endowed Institute for Radium Research. At the Second Physics Institute next door, Blau did her doctoral research to explain observations of the absorption of divergent gamma rays, high-energy, massless radiation emitted from the nucleus during radioactive decay. Blau's paper on the topic appeared in the proceedings of the Imperial Academy of Sciences. She received her PhD degree in 1919.

In 1918, World War I ended in a German and Austrian defeat. The Austro-Hungarian empire was dismantled, and Vienna, no longer the capital of an empire of fifty-three million, became the capital of a weak and impoverished republic of six and a half million. Hunger was widespread, and political turmoil and anti-Semitism flourished. One of Blau's brothers renounced Judaism and legally declared himself an atheist; two of her uncles were baptized as Christians and changed their names. Marietta Blau did not renounce her Jewish heritage.

Late in 1919, Blau's father died after a brief illness. At the time, Marietta was training doctors in X-ray techniques at the X-ray institute of Vienna's general hospital. Two years later, she found employment as a physicist in an X-ray tube factory. She wrote to Stefan Meyer, her thesis professor, "The work has been very agreeable up to now; I mainly deal with X-rays and ultraviolet light. However, I am quite exhausted because I have to work in the laboratory from 8 a.m. to 5:30 p.m. with only half an hour for lunch." Blau was still not robust. She was only a fraction over five feet tall, and throughout her life, those who met her commented on her fragile appearance.

In 1922, Blau took a position as an assistant professor at the University of Frankfurt. There she led scientific investigations for industry and provided X-ray training for physicians and doctoral students. However, when her mother fell ill the following year, Blau resigned her position and returned to Vienna, where she exchanged her paid position for volunteer work at the Institute for Radium Research. Caring for her mother became an important focus of her life for several decades. The support was mutual, with her mother supervising their household and relieving Marietta of many tasks of everyday life that she found daunting.

During the fifteen years that Blau worked at the Radium Institute, over one third of the staff were women, many of them unpaid volunteers. Funding for research was low and dropping under the conservative government. However, Stefan Meyer, director of the Institute, was particularly welcoming to women. He saw his researchers as allies, not subordinates, and he created an atmosphere among them of friendly mutual support. Meyer was Jewish, and for a while the Institute also provided shelter against the anti-Semitism rising elsewhere in Austria, where during the 1920s students sometimes shouted down Jewish professors or ejected Jewish students from lecture halls. A representative of the Catholic Student Union who later became Chancellor of Austria wrote in 1920,

> *We want to preserve our rights as masters of the house and do not want to be pushed aside by one foreign people, one foreign race. While we adhere strictly to the principles of German hospitality, we have to protect ourselves and bar all those parasites who are intruding upon us . . . and are beginning to outnumber us . . . All Jews from the East have to be removed and those who are responsible for this situation, the so-called local Jews, restricted to their rights . . .*

In this atmosphere, Blau and others often felt insecure.

In 1924, Blau published a paper on the radioactive decay of a polonium isotope. Then, at Stefan Meyer's suggestion, she turned her attention to using photographic plates to detect particles emitted in nuclear interactions. At the time, such particles were detected using the scintillation method. Ionizing radiation causes weak flashes of light on certain kinds of screens, and a researcher in a dark room, peering through a microscope, could count the flashes as they occurred. But the scintillation method was observer-dependent and subject to error. A photographic system, by contrast, would create a permanent record. When silver bromide crystals in emulsion are struck by light or higher-energy radiation such as X-rays, gamma rays, or radioactive particles, individual silver atoms are released to form an image.

As she worked on improving photographic emulsions, Blau's health continued to trouble her. In 1929 she again spent some time in a sanatorium. She emerged still an avid smoker. Like other women who handled radiochemicals in test tubes, she also suffered blistering burns to her fingertips, which caused her recurring pain all her life.

Between 1925 and 1932, Blau published a series of papers on the photographic capture of radiation. She worked out how to distinguish tracks made by protons from those made by alpha particles, which consist of two protons and two neutrons. In 1928, Blau began supervising the doctoral research of Hertha Wambacher, who in contrast to the tiny Blau was tall, robust, blonde, and loud. Wambacher completed her thesis in 1930 and received her PhD in 1932. Two years later, Wambacher joined the National Socialist German Workers (Nazi) Party, but the two women continued to work well together for another four years. They shared a medal from the Photographic Society of Vienna and consulted with the Agfa film company.

During the earliest manned balloon flights, the balloon remained tethered to the ground for safety. The first untethered flight took place on November 21, 1783, in Paris. Soon balloons became popular for adventurous outings, military surveillance, and scientific research.

Dmitri Mendeleev, creator of the periodic table of the elements, took a solo flight in a hydrogen balloon on a cloudy day in 1887 in order to observe a solar eclipse. In 1935, balloonists Orvil Anderson and Albert Stevens became the first people to directly observe the curvature of the earth, from a height of fourteen miles.

Today, high-altitude balloon flights continue to be used to study the atmosphere, weather, and cosmic rays. Helium balloons packed with instruments, usually unmanned, transmit their findings to the earth's surface. Unmanned balloons are especially useful in the upper atmosphere, far above where planes can fly but, because of the atmosphere's drag, too low for satellites.

HESS IN HIS BALLOON, NEW YORK TIMES

In 1932, Blau received a research fellowship that allowed her to work first in Göttingen—which she called "dreadfully bureaucratic"—and then at the Curie Institute in Paris, where she liked all three principals, Marie Curie, her daughter Irène, and Irène's husband Frédéric Joliot. "The only unpleasant side of Paris," she wrote to Meyer, "is that one is not allowed to smoke in the Curie Institute. The only one who does smoke is Joliot, but when his wife sees him doing so, she gets very annoyed." Blau gave colloquia and collaborated at both institutes, exhibiting a confidence in interacting with top researchers that belied her usual shyness. Still, after her sojourn in Paris she decided not to return to Germany, where Hitler had just become Reich Chancellor, the head of the German government.

Back in Austria, Blau supervised five doctoral students. In 1937, she and Wambacher were awarded the Lieben Prize of the Vienna Academy of Sciences "for their study of the photographic effects of radiation, protons and neutrons." By that time Blau was in pursuit of something more elusive: she wanted to capture photographic evidence of cosmic rays.

*"A radiation of very great penetrating power
enters our atmosphere from above."*
-Victor Hess

Cosmic rays are nuclear particles, usually protons or whole nuclei, whose origin lies outside the solar system in supernovae or the centers of galaxies. They have tremendously high energy and travel at nearly the speed of light. In 1912, Victor Hess, using an electroscope, showed in a balloon flight that higher levels of ionizing radiation existed the higher one went in the atmosphere. Hess, who won a Nobel Prize in 1936 for his work, wrote, "The results of my observation are best explained by the assumption that a radiation of very great penetrating power enters our atmosphere from above." Robert Millikan gave the new radiation the name "cosmic rays" without knowing that they were actually high energy particles.

By the 1930s, cosmic rays were routinely measured using ionization chambers, but like the scintillation method, these did not leave a permanent trace. In 1937, in the mountaintop observatory at Hafelekar, Blau and Wambacher exposed a set of specially prepared photographic plates for several months. To their delight, they finally detected a new set of tracks that looked like tiny exploding stars. These were the tracks that resulted when a cosmic particle struck another nucleus, and the resulting nuclear reaction sent particles flying in all directions. Blau was able to analyze these traces, called disintegration stars, to determine the reactions and the energy of the incoming particles. Excited, Blau and Wambacher published their findings in *Nature* and immediately began a new set of experiments, wrapping their photographic plates in foil to block alpha and beta radiation and sending the plates to various elevations, including balloon flights. As Blau later wrote, "All this was interrupted, however, by the political events in Austria in 1938."

HAFELEKAR, WHERE BLAU AND WAMBACKER FIRST CAUGHT IMAGES OF COSMIC RAYS

JEWS FORCED TO SCRUB THE STREETS OF VIENNA
IMMEDIATELY AFTER THE ANSCHLUSS

Despite the progress in their research, relations between the Nazi party member Wambacher and her Jewish mentor were rapidly deteriorating. A professor friend named Ellen Gleditch wrote to a mutual friend, "I can tell you that Dr. Blau has been abominably treated by the Nazis and among them Dr. W." Albert Einstein, impressed by Blau's photographic studies and concerned about her safety, worked to find her a position in Mexico, thinking that an emerging nation could well accommodate her relatively equipment-light research. Meanwhile, Blau left Vienna on March 12, heading for conferences in Copenhagen and Oslo. By chance, on that day the *Anschluss*, Germany's lightning annexation of Austria, began. Blau wrote that she "perhaps was the last Austrian to pass the German border. In Vienna, we did not know what lay ahead until the last moment, and it was only on my trip that I met the German troops and realized that all hope was gone. I don't know now whether I will ever return or will be treated as a refugee." Distraught, she gave a faltering talk at Bohr's institute in Copenhagen. She reported that everyone was very kind to her, but she

*"I met the German troops
and realized that all hope was gone."*

felt panicky at the thought of her mother left behind and unprotected in Vienna.

Physicists throughout Germany and Austria were losing their jobs. Stefan Meyer resigned as director of the Radium Institute and found himself shunted aside by people he had nurtured. Not only Jews but any physicists who opposed the Nazi regime lost their positions. Hertha Wambacher flourished. Einstein tried to get Blau a position in America, but the market was flooded with German physicists seeking refuge, and the economy was still only slowly recovering from the Depression. Within a few months, however, Einstein's Mexican efforts bore fruit, and Blau was offered a position teaching advanced students at the Technical University in Mexico City. First, though, she had to get a new passport, since her Austrian passport belonged to a country that no longer existed. With her new German passport, stamped with a J, she flew through Hamburg to London, where she met her mother. During the Hamburg stopover, she was searched and all her research notes were confiscated. Her younger colleague Berta Karlik wrote to Gleditch, "I can't help feeling that there is something rather pathetic about this poor little frail figure, so utterly worn out by one blow after another, now crossing the ocean to start a new life in what still seems to me a somewhat exotic country."

On January 1, 1939, Blau began work in Mexico City. She strove to learn Spanish and fretted over the lack of decent equipment, even microscopes. She built Geiger counters and sent her students on trips to mountains, including the volcano Popocatepetl, to expose photographic plates. She also turned her mind to various practical questions, such as calculating the theoretical effect of solar radiation on the health of the Mexican people, many of whom lived at high altitude in a tropical zone. The presence of volcanoes and frequent earthquakes also piqued her interest in the earth's crust. During her five years in Mexico, she published seven papers on various topics, but none in her area of primary expertise.

Meanwhile, Blau's mother Florentine, with the help of a maid and the company of a chihuahua, ran their

As World War II began, Mexico, worn out by its own wars and the Depression, remained neutral. Many Mexican communists wanted to side with Germany, which was initially allied with Russia. In 1941, when Germany invaded Russia, they changed their minds. Still, historical resentment against the United States remained high.

When Japan attacked Pearl Harbor, Mexico pledged its support to its northern neighbor and cut off diplomatic ties with the Axis powers. The U.S. sent technicians to mine key Mexican ores such as mercury, zinc, and copper, and Mexican oil supplied American planes and warships. The two countries officially agreed on a program for Mexican farmworkers to work in American fields. Thousands of Mexican immigrants joined the American armed forces to fight in Europe and Japan.

In 1942, after German submarines began sinking Mexican merchant ships and oil tankers, Mexico declared war on the Axis powers. The Mexican navy fought German ships, and the 201st Air Squadron of three hundred airmen, called the "Aztec Eagles," fought beside the U.S. Air Force in the Philippines.

home. Socially, the Blaus avoided the large number of pro-Nazi Germans in Mexico City. Instead, they joined a group of patriotic Austrian exiles who published a monthly journal called *Austria Libre* and held frequent cultural events. Blau attended concerts and lectures, and she herself lectured on the Mexican sun. In 1942, when Mexico joined the war against the Axis powers, Blau wrote with uncharacteristic vehemence, "I would be happy to get personally involved in the war and stand behind a cannon or get shot as a human torpedo against a German ship, but they won't take me." She wished she could at least join a war industry, but there was no opportunity to do so in Mexico.

Meanwhile the Radium Institute in Vienna, purged of Jewish researchers, focused its research on nuclear fission. Hertha Wambacher became closely allied with Georg Stetter, the newly appointed Nazi director of neutron research. Wambacher continued to publish on the topic of nuclear reactions induced by cosmic rays, and she rose through the hierarchy, eventually becoming a professor. In her work she made no mention of her onetime mentor and collaborator.

In 1943, Florentine Blau died of liver cancer. The loss of Blau's mother was a painful blow, and only weeks later, Blau herself fell ill with typhus. Once she recovered, she realized that without her mother to care for, she was now more mobile. In 1944, having received permission to immigrate to the United States, she moved to New York City, where her brother Ludwig was living, and took a job in industry. There she worked on devising instruments for measuring radiation and researching the use of radioactivity in manufacturing. She published in scientific journals and filed for several patents, but she found the work dull. When in 1947, Blau was transferred to a small town in Wisconsin, she found the move almost unbearable. Single, a foreigner, unable to drive, she was isolated and bored. She wrote to colleagues, companies, and universities in search of another job.

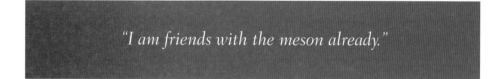

"I am friends with the meson already."

Finally, Columbia University offered her a position as staff scientist with a salary of $7200 a year. Delighted, Blau moved back to New York City. She was assigned to improve the photographic emulsion process for the study of high-energy particles. New particle accelerators, with names like the Cosmotron and the Bevatron, generated particles that were replacing cosmic rays as objects of study. Delighted to be back at work in her area of expertise, Blau wrote to Stefan Meyer, "I have to get acquainted with the new physics, but I am friends with the meson already." With an old Vienna colleague, she developed a way of evaluating emulsion results that could be semi-automated, allowing researchers to process voluminous results far more quickly.

In 1950, now a naturalized American citizen, Blau began to work at the Brookhaven National Laboratory on Long Island. Finally working with the most advanced equipment, she used her emulsions to study the interaction of high-energy protons with light and heavy elements. That same year, the Nobel Prize in Physics was awarded to Cecil F. Powell "for his development of the

WILSON CLOUD CHAMBER AT BROOKHAVEN
NATIONAL LABORATORY

PHYSICS

photographic method of studying nuclear processes and his discoveries regarding mesons made with this method." Erwin Schrödinger had actually nominated Blau and Wambacher for the prize based on their work before 1938, but, perhaps because their discoveries did not fundamentally advance the field of nuclear physics, the Nobel committee passed over the two women. Powell, the winner, began his work after 1938, and in 1946 he detected the tracks of pi mesons in photographic plates exposed to cosmic rays. In his Nobel acceptance speech, Powell did not mention Blau or Wambacher, but in an autobiographical note in 1970, he wrote that reading about Blau and Wambacher's work had encouraged him to explore the use of photographic plates.

At Brookhaven, Blau's research demonstrated new findings about collisions using mesons. The atmosphere at Brookhaven was more competitive than collaborative, and after five years Blau began to find it tiring. In 1955, at age sixty-one, she accepted a position as associate professor at the University of Miami. Driving to Florida, she found herself "deeply touched and saddened," to encounter the open discrimination suffered by blacks in the South. In Florida, she collected equipment and soon began productive collaborations with a number of colleagues. With her post-doctoral student Arnold Perlmutter, she published a series of articles on kappa and negative pi mesons. Perlmutter later wrote of her:

Belying her tiny stature and gentle and self-effacing demeanor, Marietta was a tenacious scientist, strong administrator and inspiring teacher. In addition, she was an exceptionally warm and cultured person, establishing close ties with her coworkers and students. She was pivotal in my life, changing the direction of my intellectual interests, acting almost as a surrogate mother and grandmother to me and my children.

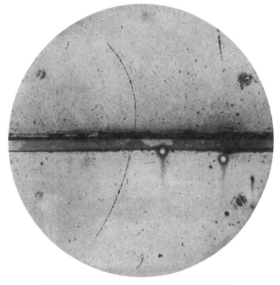

SUBATOMIC PARTICLE BENDING TRACK
THROUGH CLOUD CHAMBER

In 1957, Erwin Schrödinger arranged for Blau to receive the Leibniz Medal of the German Academy of Sciences in Berlin. Blau was delighted, but could not accept the medal because it was issued in East Germany, with which the United States had no diplomatic relations. Two years later she was granted the medal again, and once more was instructed by the State Department to turn it down. By then, Blau was suffering from cataracts and angina, chest pain caused by insufficient circulation to the heart muscle. Her health worsened when she fell down her garden stairs and broke her arm. Friends and colleagues helped care for her, but Blau had already decided to return at last to Vienna. Only there could she afford the cataract surgery she needed.

In 1960, after a twenty-two year absence, Marietta Blau returned to the city of her birth. She rented a small apartment, delighted in musical performances, and managed to live comfortably on her pension of two hundred dollars a month. Due to the advocacy of some of her old colleagues, she was awarded the Schrödinger Prize in 1962. At the Radium Institute, Blau was given a small office and immediately volunteered as an advisor to the high-energy physics group. She turned down a paid position to lead the group, not feeling well enough to work full time, but she did take on a couple of young women as doctoral students. She gave talks and lectures and contributed chapters to a book on experimental techniques edited by Chien-Shiung Wu.

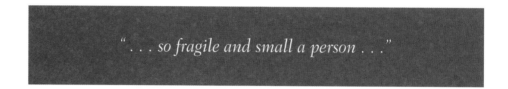

". . . so fragile and small a person . . ."

In Vienna, Blau was once again lonely. The breach between those who had thrived during the war and those who had fled for their lives, losing almost everything, never fully healed. Although she grew close to her students, Blau said very little about how she came to emigrate. Colleagues described her as distant and guarded. However, her students found her generous and unpretentious. Her student Gerta Haider wrote, "She was small and slight and had enormous dark eyes and very strong glasses, which made her eyes appear even larger. Often she appeared rather helpless to me . . . She was something like a surrogate mother to me . . . and helped me out in my private life." A visitor to the lab wrote, "I was surprised that so fragile and small a person with such a soft, shy voice could exude such authority."

By the end of 1964, when Gerda Haider received her PhD, Blau could no longer walk long distances, and she quit her activities at the Radium Institute. Ill health kept her mostly at home for the next several years. In 1969, fifty years after receiving her doctorate, she received an honorary renewal of her doctoral degree. That same year, a tumor was found in her lung. After four months in the hospital, she died of lung cancer on January 27, 1970. Berta Karlik, head of the Radium Institute, meant to write her scientific obituary for *Acta Physica Austraica*, but she fell ill herself and never got around to writing it. In fact, no scientific journal noted Marietta Blau's passing.

Like Lise Meitner and Emmy Noether, Marietta Blau was a woman who overcame educational and institutional barriers to become an internationally respected researcher, only to find herself exiled by the cruelly racist policies of National Socialism. A shy and sheltered person who was never at ease navigating the demands of practical life, she was forced to move multiple times, rebuilding her work and her scientific identity each time. After she left Vienna, she never again had the privilege of working in a close, collaborative group of scientific colleagues. Perhaps because of her constant relocation and limited equipment, her work focused on improving research techniques more than on making foundational discoveries. Still, wherever she went, she quietly established her competence. She took pleasure in mentoring young researchers with the same kindness and generosity Stefan Meyer had shown her. She was happiest when working closely with physics colleagues, no matter their nationality. During her lifetime, although she was three times nominated for a Nobel Prize, her accomplishments were overshadowed and sometimes suppressed. In recent years, however, she has begun to receive recognition as one of the pioneers of emulsion physics and the measurement of particle interactions.

PHYSICS

Timeline | 1896-1957

Gerty Radnitz, later Cori, | 1896
born in Prague

1900 | Height of Art
Nouveau style

ZODIAC BY
ALPHONSE MUCHA

World War I | 1914-1918 ..... 1914 | Enters medical school

Carl and Gerty Cori marry | 1920 ..... 1918 | Czechoslovakia becomes
and publish first research paper a republic

Work out the Cori cycle | 1922-1928 ..... 1922 | Move to New York
of glucose metabolism

Move to Washington University | 1931 ..... 1930 | Chrysler Building
of St. Louis completed in
New York City

Prohibition ends | 1933

CHRYSLER
BUILDING

DUMPING ALCOHOL
DURING PROHIBITION

1939-1945 | World War II

1943 | Becomes associate research professor
of biochemistry

Coris win Nobel Prize; Gerty | 1947 ..... 1948 | Czechoslovakia becomes a communist
diagnosed with bone marrow disease state in orbit of USSR

Korean War | 1950-1953 ..... 1951-1952 | Identifies first enzyme defects in
glycogen storage diseases

1956 | Elvis Presley's
"Hound Dog"

Death of | 1957 ..... tops the charts
Gerty Cori

CIVILIANS IN THE
KOREAN WAR

ELVIS PRESLEY STAMP

9 | *Energy Cycle*

Gerty Cori

1896-1957 | *Austro-Hungarian Empire and United States*

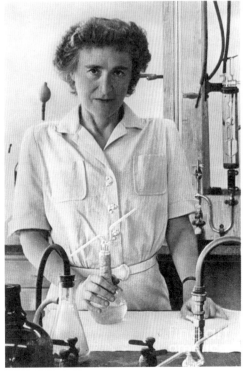

GERTY CORI

At the start of the twentieth century, nobody knew exactly how animals turned food into movement. How was food stored for energy, and how was that energy released to help muscles contract? Beginning in the 1920s, one of the most remarkable couples in the history of science, Gerty and Carl Cori, worked out the answer. They isolated the enzymes and delineated the steps involved in how sugar is stored in the liver as starch and then released for use in the muscles. The cycle they discovered, one of the first and most fundamental biochemical pathways to be worked out in detail, bears their name: the Cori cycle.

Gerty Theresa Radnitz was born to a distinguished Jewish family on August 15, 1896, in Prague, then part of the Austro-Hungarian Empire. Her father was a chemist and a businessman who managed a set of sugar refineries. Her uncle on her mother's side was a professor of pediatrics at the University of Prague. Until the age of ten, Gerty was taught at home; then she attended a girls' school, from which she graduated in 1912. At that point her uncle encouraged her to study medicine, but her schooling had been aimed at helping her acquire the social graces a woman needed, and she lacked the required background in Latin, mathematics, physics, and chemistry. Still, she persisted. On a family holiday in the mountainous Tyrol the summer she was sixteen, she met a high school teacher who volunteered to tutor her in Latin. Applying herself, Gerty mastered three years of Latin that summer. The next year she entered a gymnasium, or academic high school, to catch up in the other missing subjects, and two years later she passed the university entrance exam.

At age eighteen, Gerty entered the Carl Ferdinand University of Prague to study medicine. During her first year, she became fascinated by the new field of biochemistry, which uses the tools of chemistry to investigate biological problems. That same year, in anatomy class, she met Carl Cori, a tall, fair-haired Catholic who like Gerty was from Prague. Carl, somewhat shy and slow of speech, was captivated by Gerty's "charm, vitality, intelligence, a sense of humor and love of the outdoors," as he later wrote. The two medical students studied, explored the mountains on foot, and skied together. But World War I was underway, and soon Carl was drafted into the ski corps and then the sanitation corps of the Austro-Hungarian army. When he returned, the two medical students collaborated in researching a component of blood. In 1920, the same year they graduated from medical school, they published their first research paper together. With that done, Gerty

COPPER ENGRAVING (1815) OF TWO YOUNG MEN WITH
CONGENITAL THYROID DEFICIENCY OR CRETINISM

Radnitz converted to Catholicism so that she could marry Carl. Against the wishes of his family, they did marry later that year.

The newly married couple worked briefly in clinics in Vienna, where Carl's preceptor was, in his words, "a brilliant but amoral physician who was strongly anti-Semitic." Soon the Coris left the clinics to take up research jobs in separate cities. Carl found a position at Graz University, where he had to prove he was not Jewish before he was hired—particularly ironic since his research mentor Otto Loewi, a brilliant scientist who later won the Nobel Prize, was himself Jewish. Carl studied the effect of the vagus nerve on the heart, while Gerty worked at the Karolinen Children's Hospital in Vienna, researching thyroid hormone. Congenital deficiency of thyroid hormone leads to short stature and mental retardation in children, a condition then called cretinism. Over the next two years, Gerty published several papers. As part of her hospital pay, she received free dinners, but the food at the hospital was so poor that she developed xerophthalmia, a dryness of the eyes caused by Vitamin A deficiency that can lead to blindness. Luckily, on a visit home to Prague, she ate well enough to cure the condition.

Concerned that Gerty's Jewish birth would hobble both their careers, and indeed that another war might be coming soon, the Coris decided to leave Europe. In 1922, Carl was offered a position running the chemistry laboratory at a Buffalo hospital, the New York State Institute for the Study of Malignant Diseases, later Roswell Park. Six months later, Gerty joined him as an assistant pathologist. She wrote later, "I believe that the benefits of two civilizations, a European education followed by the freedom and opportunities of this country, have been essential to whatever contributions I have been able to make to science."

Laboratory duties were light at Roswell Park, and the equipment was advanced. The Coris soon began to pursue their own research on the side. Gerty published four papers on the effects of radiation on stained and unstained skin and on the metabolism of different body organs. It is possible that excessive exposure to radiation in 1923 and 1924 contributed to the blood disorder that later killed her.

Soon the Coris began to work together on carbohydrate metabolism, how the body breaks down and uses the starches and sugars we eat. They worked meticulously, developing methods to measure the amounts of glucose, glycogen, lactic acid, and phosphates in the blood. Meanwhile, they had to avoid interference from the institute director, who liked to add his name to their manuscripts without reading them, and who insisted that cancer was caused by parasites. At one point he warned Gerty to keep to her own laboratory and stop working with Carl or else lose her job. She did not obey for long.

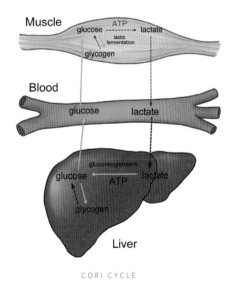

CORI CYCLE

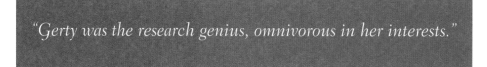

"Gerty was the research genius, omnivorous in her interests."

Over six years of careful research, the Coris worked out the basics of how mammals turn glycogen in the liver into glucose in the blood; how that glucose is "burned" into energy and lactic acid in the muscle; and how in the presence of oxygen the lactic acid is reprocessed into glucose and then to glycogen once more in the liver. The cycle varies depending on the presence or absence of oxygen, and it has branches and subreactions that the Coris spent the rest of their research lives refining. They worked well together, sometimes clashing because of the strength of their ideas. "Carl was the visionary," wrote one research associate later. "Gerty was the research genius, omnivorous in her interests . . . Gerty read enormously widely and deeply. She was his initial processor, and he got many of his ideas from her outreach." The Coris published fifty joint research papers during their years in Buffalo, with whichever of them had done the major work listed first. In addition, Gerty published eleven solo papers.

The elucidation of the cycle of glucose metabolism, which quickly became known as the Cori cycle, helped at once with the management of diabetes. Insulin had been discovered in 1921, but the Cori cycle explained how the body normally maintains a nearly constant blood level of glucose between meals.

In 1928, the Coris became naturalized United States citizens. By that time, Carl was receiving job offers from a number of universities. Gerty, at least his equal in productivity, received no offers. Moreover, in most universities, nepotism rules meant Gerty could not get a job in the same institution as her husband, a condition that made Carl turn most offers down. Finally, in 1931, the Washington University of St. Louis School of

GERTY AND CARL CORI IN THE LAB, 1947.
FROM THE SMITHSONIAN INSTITUTION.

*In 1915, Dr. Walter Cannon introduced the phrase "**fight or flight response**" to explain what happens in the body of a mammal that becomes frightened or enraged. The animal's pupils dilate and its muscles tense. Its heart rate and blood pressure rise. The blood vessels feeding its muscles dilate, and its breathing becomes deeper and faster.*

The fight or flight response begins deep in the brain, in the amygdala. Signals from the amygdala trigger responses in the hypothalamus and the pituitary gland, which releases a hormone called ACTH. ACTH activates the adrenal glands to release both cortisol and epinephrine. Epinephrine binds to liver cells, leading them to release glucose, while ACTH works to make fatty acids available as energy. Epinephrine and nor-epinephrine also act on the heart, blood vessels, and smooth muscle throughout the body.

Together, these changes almost immediately increase blood flow and the delivery of oxygen and glucose to muscles, allowing the animal to respond to the emergency with a sudden increase in strength and speed.

WALTER CANNON

Medicine appointed Carl chair of the department of pharmacology, while allowing him to hire Gerty as a research assistant. Her salary, at fifteen hundred dollars, was one-fifth of her husband's, but at least they were able to continue working together. In St. Louis the pair continued their studies on glucose metabolism, focusing on how epinephrine, a natural hormone released by the adrenal glands, causes glycogen in muscle to break down into glucose, which can be used in the "fight or flight" response. The Coris kept simplifying their research system, working first with whole animals, then muscles, then small slices of muscle, and finally with cells that had been broken open.

As part of their work on glucose metabolism, the Coris continued to find new enzymes, which are proteins that catalyze reactions. Each enzyme had a specific, precise role. Other researchers joined the laboratory, and in the 1940s it became one of the world's most active centers for discovering new enzymes. In all, six future Nobel Prize winners, besides the Coris themselves, passed through the laboratory as visiting researchers.

Gerty ran the laboratory with a fierce attention to quality and precision. Everyone who joined the team had to learn her procedures for preparing reagents and performing experiments. Her student and collaborator Joseph Larner remembered that although he had already published in a prestigious journal by the time he joined her group, "she personally taught me how to pipette, watched over my shoulder as I performed my first standard curve for the analysis of glucose, [and] taught me how to crystallize muscle phosphorylase." She washed her own laboratory glassware. She was careless only with the cigarettes she constantly smoked, letting ashes fall on the laboratory benches.

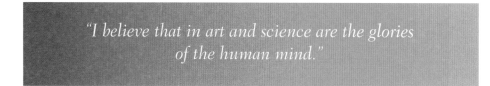

"I believe that in art and science are the glories of the human mind."

Both Coris read voraciously, both at work and at home. Gerty somehow convinced the medical library to deliver the newest issues of any relevant journal to her before placing them on the shelves. She tore through the journal articles, picking up ideas. She also had the local library deliver five books to her each week and then pick them up the next week while delivering her newest order. The Coris liked to read aloud to each other at home, and their conversation was erudite and informed on a broad range of topics, from art and literature to political theory and science. Broad exposure to culture helped sustain both Coris. In her contribution to Edwin R. Murrow's "This I Believe" radio series, Gerty wrote,

> *I believe that in art and science are the glories of the human mind. I see no conflict between them. In the past they have flourished together during the great and happy periods of history . . . Contemplation of the great human achievements through the ages is helpful to me in moments of despair and doubt. Human meanness and folly then seem less important.*

In 1936 Gerty, at the age of forty, had a son whom they named Tom Carl Cori. Three days later, Gerty was back at work. Tom grew up a typical baseball-loving American boy, not as studious as his parents would have liked. They clashed with him often during his adolescence, but in the end he became a PhD chemist and head of a chemical supply company.

In 1943, Gerty was promoted to research associate professor of biochemistry. Four years later she finally became a full professor with tenure and a significant salary. That same year, she and Carl, along with Bernardo Alberto Houssay of Argentina, shared the Nobel Prize. The Coris' share of the prize was awarded for their discoveries of glycogen and glucose metabolism. The prize citation read, in part, "Your synthesis of glycogen in the test tube is beyond doubt one of the most brilliant achievements in modern biochemistry."

Just before leaving for Stockholm, Gerty received devastating news. She had been hiking in Snowmass, Colorado when she fainted at high altitude. She assumed the cause was anemia and consulted her doctor. His diagnosis was agnogenic myeloid dysplasia, also called myelofibrosis. Her bone marrow was gradually being replaced by fibrous tissue, and she was no longer making red blood cells. Only regular transfusions would keep her alive.

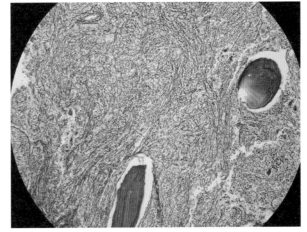

MYELOFIBROSIS IN THE BONE MARROW. NOTE THE STAINED FIBERS AND FEW BLOOD CELLS

Still, the Coris went off to Stockholm to collect the prize and took a side trip through Europe as though nothing had happened. On their return home, they shared the monetary prize with several co-workers. Then they went back to work. For ten years, Carl Cori monitored his wife's hemoglobin levels and administered blood transfusions to her every couple of weeks. She kept working, only setting up a cot in her office so she could lie down and read journals when she needed to rest. However, as the years went on, Gerty began to have more serious reactions to the transfusions, which contained white as well as red blood cells. She felt sick and feverish after every transfusion.

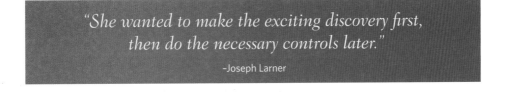

*"She wanted to make the exciting discovery first,
then do the necessary controls later."*

–Joseph Larner

Nevertheless, Gerty never let discouragement over the course of her sickness spill over into her work. Joseph Larner, who worked with her during her illness, wrote,

> *Gerty had a vivacity and a love of science and discovery that were infectious. She wanted to make the exciting discovery first, then do the necessary controls later. She and Carl had an instinctive "feel" for the right path to follow to solve the problem. She needed only one exciting experimental finding to jump into a problem with unbounded energy.*

When some experiment gave a pleasing result, she would go running down the hallway in her heels, clickety-clacking and calling out, "Carlie! Carlie!" so they could share the excitement right away.

*After World War II, American leaders sought to continue the level of research that had led to radar, penicillin, and the atom bomb. In 1950, an Act of Congress established the **National Science Foundation** (NSF) to support research and education in science and engineering. The Foundation issued its first grants and fellowships in 1952.*

Over the years, the NSF has funded computer science research, established astronomical observatories and a South Pole station, and pioneered deep ocean exploration. Its grants have equipped research institutions and schools. It has supported efforts to improve science curriculum and teaching at all levels. NSF-supported research has led to advances in areas as diverse as speech recognition technology, drug discovery, nanoscience, understanding the dangers of icing on aircraft, and documenting rare languages before they disappear.

In the years after receiving the Nobel Prize, Gerty attacked a new problem, glycogen storage diseases in children. In this class of congenital diseases, glycogen accumulates in muscle, liver, or other tissues, leading to slowed growth, delayed development, low blood sugar, and often death in childhood. Gerty and Larner made a bet as to which enzyme was involved. Both were right: Gerty soon identified four different forms of the disease based on defects in four different enzymes. She was tremendously excited by the results. For the first time since sickle cell anemia, a specific molecular defect could be shown to cause a disease, and this was first time a disease had been traced to a defect in an enzyme. To be able to make a genetic diagnosis by analyzing a small piece of liver from a biopsy represented a significant advance. Today, eleven glycogen storage diseases are known, some of which can be treated with a special diet.

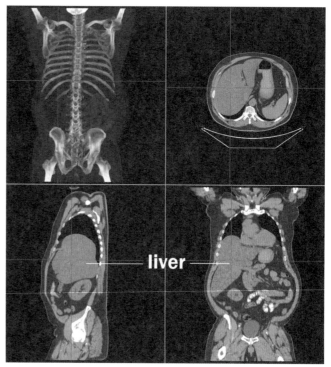

AN ENLARGED LIVER CROWDS BOTH THE LUNGS AND THE ABDOMINAL ORGANS IN THIS CT SCAN OF A CHILD WITH A GLYCOGEN STORAGE DISEASE.

After receiving the Nobel Prize, Gerty Cori was elected to the National Academy of Sciences, eight years after her husband. President Truman appointed her to the newly formed board of the National Science Foundation. Before each meeting, she primed herself with a large transfusion to give her strength for the airplane flight to Washington, D.C. But Gerty gradually weakened. She fought angrily against her frailty, firing the nurses Carl hired to care for her. In the summer of 1957, she published her last article. Soon Carl was carrying her from room to room in the laboratory; then she was bedridden at home. She died at home on October 26, 1957, at age sixty-one, having continued to do cutting-edge science until the end. Carl was by her side, as he had been throughout their long and immensely productive working life.

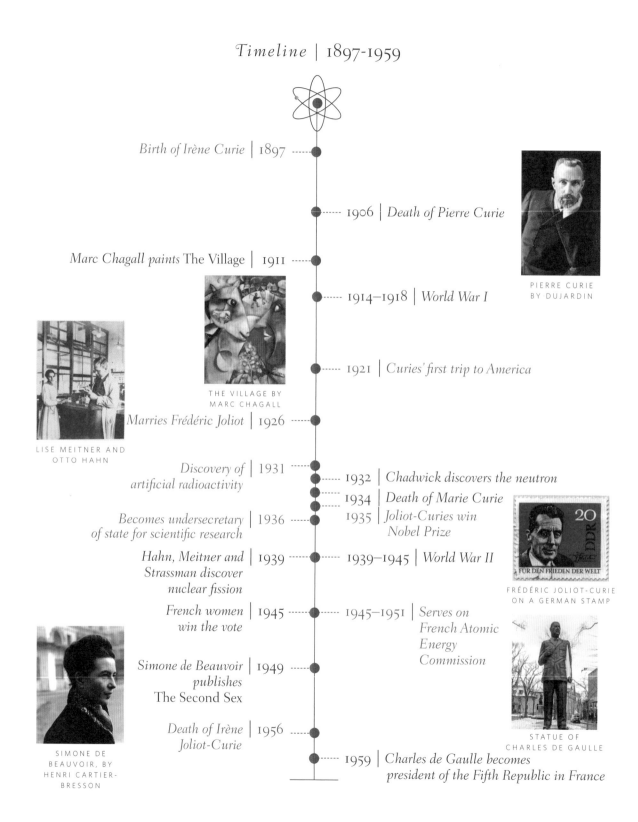

Timeline | 1897-1959

Birth of Irène Curie | 1897

1906 | Death of Pierre Curie

Marc Chagall paints The Village | 1911

1914–1918 | World War I

1921 | Curies' first trip to America

Marries Frédéric Joliot | 1926

Discovery of | 1931
artificial radioactivity

1932 | Chadwick discovers the neutron

1934 | Death of Marie Curie

Becomes undersecretary | 1936
of state for scientific research

1935 | Joliot-Curies win
Nobel Prize

Hahn, Meitner and | 1939
Strassman discover
nuclear fission

1939–1945 | World War II

French women | 1945
win the vote

1945–1951 | Serves on
French Atomic
Energy
Commission

Simone de Beauvoir | 1949
publishes
The Second Sex

Death of Irène | 1956
Joliot-Curie

1959 | Charles de Gaulle becomes
president of the Fifth Republic in France

PIERRE CURIE
BY DUJARDIN

THE VILLAGE BY
MARC CHAGALL

LISE MEITNER AND
OTTO HAHN

FRÉDÉRIC JOLIOT-CURIE
ON A GERMAN STAMP

STATUE OF
CHARLES DE GAULLE

SIMONE DE
BEAUVOIR, BY
HENRI CARTIER-
BRESSON

10 | *Artificial Radiation*

Irène Joliot-Curie

1897-1956 | *France*

In many ways, Irène Joliot-Curie's life echoed that of her mother, the famous physicist Marie Curie. Like Marie, Irène lost a parent at an early age, married a fellow scientist, won a Nobel Prize with her husband, taught at the Sorbonne, was refused admission to the French Academy of Sciences, and died of a radiation-induced blood disease. Calm and dedicated, Irène never appeared daunted by her parents' fame. She freely chose her life in physics. "That one must do some work seriously and must be independent and not merely amuse oneself in life—this our mother has told us always, but never that science was the only career worth following," she said.

> *"One must do some work seriously and must be independent and not merely amuse oneself."*

Irène Curie was born one month prematurely on September 12, 1897, in Paris, just after her parents returned from a long bicycle ride. In 1897, Marie Curie was just beginning the study of uranium rays that would lead to her great discoveries. To help care for the baby while her parents spent long hours in the laboratory, Pierre's father, Dr. Eugène Curie, came to live with the family. Irène adored him. He taught her about nature and introduced her to the socialist ideals she carried through her life.

Marie carefully recorded Irène's growth and development. On vacations in Brittany, Irène's father Pierre took her on walks or bicycle rides, pointing out plants and animals and talking to her about mathematics. Both parents believed that children's education should include plenty of fresh air and exercise.

When Irène was six years old, her parents won the Nobel Prize in Physics for their discovery of radioactivity, although they did not travel to Stockholm to collect the prize for another two years. Irène's sister Eve, who grew up to be a talented musician and writer with no interest in science, was born the year after the Nobel award.

Two years after Eve's birth, when Irène was nine years old, their father Pierre was killed in a sudden accident, run over in the street by a heavy, horse-drawn cart. Their mother took over teaching Pierre's course in physics at the Sorbonne. Otherwise she withdrew into mourning and did little but go to her laboratory and visit the cemetery in the nearby village of Sceaux. Eventually she moved the family into the village to be closer to the cemetery.

Once in Sceaux, Marie pulled herself together enough to help organize a cooperative school with other Sorbonne professors, including Pierre's former student, Paul Langevin. Eminent scholars taught each other's children mathematics, science, Chinese, sculpture, or whatever else interested both teachers and pupils. The children were also physically active. "We did gymnastics, swimming, bicycling, horseback riding . . . we rowed, we skated," Irène remembered.

But sorrow continued to visit. At thirteen, Irène lost another father figure with the death of her beloved grandfather. The following year, scandal broke over the family when the tabloid press in Paris published a series of letters, perhaps partly forged, between the widowed Marie Curie and the married Paul Langevin. Newspapers demanded that the "foreign" home-breaker, Marie Curie, return to her native Poland, and crowds threw rocks at the windows of the family's house. Marie and her terrified daughters sought refuge in the home of friends, Emile and Marguerite Borel.

Although Marie rallied sufficiently to journey to Stockholm to receive her second Nobel Prize, this time in chemistry, on her return she fell ill with a kidney infection worsened by a near-suicidal depression. The girls came under the care of a Polish governess and for a year and a half barely saw their mother, who lived under a pseudonym in a town close to Paris as she recovered. Sad and confused, the girls wrote longing letters to their mother. Marie, too, tried to bridge the distance with letters; she sent Irène complex math problems by mail. In one letter, the fourteen-year-old Irène, always eager

EVE, MARIE, AND IRÈNE CURIE IN 1908

MISSY MELONEY WITH IRÈNE, MARIE, AND EVE, 1921

to please her mother, wrote, "The derivatives are coming along all right, the inverse functions are adorable." Marie also urged Irène to watch over Eve, who at seven was much more inclined toward music than mathematics or science.

In the summer of 1912, still fleeing exposure, Marie and her daughters traveled incognito to stay with the English physicist Hertha Ayrton. Ayrton tutored Irène in mathematics and introduced both girls to the cause of women's rights. By December, Marie felt well enough to resume work. The family returned to Paris, and Irène enrolled in a private high school. The following summer brought another healing vacation, as the three Curies met up with Albert Einstein, his wife, and his ten-year-old son for two weeks of hiking in the Alps. Life was looking more cheerful. Soon the seventeen-year-old Irène graduated from her Paris high school and began taking physics courses at the Sorbonne. Then war came.

In June 1914, Serb nationalists assassinated the Austrian archduke Franz Ferdinand in Sarajevo. Bound by an interlocking system of often secret alliances, Europe geared itself up for war. Germany declared war on Russia, then France. Austria invaded Poland. By August 30, Germany had invaded and occupied part of the French countryside.

As France threw itself into war, Marie worked to build a mobile X-ray fleet to serve field hospitals at the front, while Irène studied nursing along with physics. Marie took Irène with her on her first trip to the battlefront in the autumn of 1914. Soon Irène was helping train nurses in X-ray techniques at her mother's new Radium Institute. Then, at the age of eighteen, she joined her mother in the field for good. Together they ran a mobile X-ray van and visited the twenty X-ray stations Marie had set up near the front. Traveling conditions were terrible and food and lodging always uncertain.

Impressed with Irène's calm competence, Marie assigned her daughter to supervise an X-ray installation in Belgium. There Irène took hundreds of X-rays and guided surgeons as they removed shrapnel or repaired broken bones. Like her mother, Irène took X-rays with no shielding, unaware that a high cumulative radiation dose could be harmful. From her contact with the sick, Irène also contracted tuberculosis, which later reactivated, causing her many years of illness. Even after the war's end, Irène continued to provide X-ray training, this time to American soldiers who were waiting to be shipped home. For her service, the French government awarded her a military medal.

IRÈNE AND MARIE, 1925

After the war, Irène returned to her studies and began research at her mother's Radium Institute. About this time, her mother's tireless efforts to equip and staff the Institute won the sympathy of an American journalist named Missy Meloney. Meloney befriended the entire family and devoted herself to their cause, enlisting the women of America to raise $100,000 to buy the Institute a gram of radium. In 1921, Irène joined her sister and mother on a grand publicity tour of the United States, including trips to Niagara Falls and the Grand Canyon. The journey ended at the White House, where President Harding symbolically presented Marie Curie with the precious gram of radium. As newsmen tailed their mother everywhere and crowds packed her lectures, Eve and Irène truly understood the extent of their mother's fame for the first time. The frail Marie, often exhausted, left many social occasions to her daughters, and Irène gave lectures and even accepted honorary degrees on her mother's behalf.

In 1925 Irène, now twenty-eight years old, completed her doctoral thesis on the alpha radiation emitted by polonium. More than a thousand people, including reporters from papers as distant as the *New York Times*, attended her thesis defense. Irène's thesis advisor, Paul Langevin, still close to the family after the traumatic events of 1911, also attended. After her lecture, Irène returned to a tea and champagne party in the garden of the Radium Institute, where Marie served drinks in laboratory flasks and beakers.

That same year, Marie assigned Irène to mentor another young protégé of Langevin's. This was Frédéric Joliot, who had graduated first in his engineering class at the Paris Municipal School of Physics and Chemistry, where he showed a gift for experimentation. At eighteen he had been drafted into the army for two years, and on his return he had won a research grant and applied to work at the Radium Institute.

> " . . . this same purity, this good sense, this tranquility."
> –Frédéric Joliot-Curie

Irène had a reputation in the lab for being remote and even unfriendly. She focused so closely on her work that she often forgot to say hello to colleagues, and when she did speak she was unfailingly blunt. Still, Joliot was determined to learn from her, so he asked her questions and insisted on walking her home at night. In some ways the two couldn't be more different. Joliot was handsome, charming, extroverted, and fun-loving, while Irène had no patience with small talk and presented a severe face to the world. But Joliot was impressed by Irène's dedication to her work and her indifference to fame, money, or personal adornment. A well-rounded athlete, Joliot also appreciated Irène's love of the outdoors and her enthusiasm for sports such as skiing. The two shared patriotic fervor, socialist sympathies, and concern for the underdog. After long walks in the countryside with Joliot, Irène wrote to a friend about him: "We have many opinions in common on essential questions." As

for Joliot, he later wrote, "In observing her I discovered in this young woman, that others saw as a little brutish, an extraordinary, poetic and sensitive being who, in a number of ways, was a living representation of her father . . . I found in his daughter this same purity, this good sense, this tranquility."

In a little over a year, Frédéric and Irène announced their intent to marry. Marie, caught by surprise, was uncertain whether the match would last. She insisted that the couple execute a prenuptial agreement specifying that after her death the Radium Institute's precious supply of radium would go to Irène alone. Then she whisked Irène away with her on a long trip to Brazil in the summer of 1926. In Brazil, Marie gave lectures while Irène performed experimental demonstrations, and the two of them hiked together in the rainforest. But whenever she could, Irène wrote to Frédéric urging him not to smoke too much or ride too fast on his motorbike.

FRÉDÉRIC JOLIOT

PHYSICS

In October, 1926, the couple married, changing both their names to Joliot-Curie. Irène quickly became pregnant. She worked in the lab up until lunchtime of the day she gave birth to her daughter Hélène. Meanwhile, Marie grew fonder of Frédéric. She wrote to a colleague, "The boy is a fireball," and insisted that he get his baccalaureate and pursue a doctoral degree. The families dined together four times a week, engaging in lively scientific and social debates.

Although both Irène and Frédéric had done good scientific work independently, once they began working together, significant research publications started pouring out of their laboratory. Foreign scientists began subscribing to French journals just to follow their work. In 1932, when Irène was pregnant with her son Pierre, she and Frédéric built on experiments by a German physicist, Walter Bothe. They placed a sample of polonium next to a bit of beryllium. The polonium emitted alpha particles, two protons and two neutrons

THE JOLIOT-CURIES IN THE LABORATORY

bound together like a helium nucleus, which bombarded the beryllium. The beryllium in turn gave off rays so powerful that they penetrated lead with no problem. When the Joliot-Curies placed paraffin wax in the way of these rays, the wax emitted fast protons traveling at a tenth the speed of light.

At the time, the neutron was unknown, and scientists thought the nucleus contained only protons and electrons. The Joliot-Curies concluded that the mystery rays from the beryllium were gamma rays, and they published their findings. Ernest Rutherford in England disagreed: how could massless gamma rays push protons to such a speed? His assistant director James Chadwick repeated the experiment and discovered the neutron, for which he won a Nobel Prize three years later.

Disappointed that they had misinterpreted their own research, the Joliot-Curies returned to their laboratory. They began using a cloud chamber to study what happened when they bombarded atoms with neutrons. Because they have no charge, neutrons are not deviated by charged particles. Still, when they collide into a nucleus, charged particles are emitted, and trails of condensing fog-like droplets show where the particles have traveled. In their photographs, Irène and Frédéric noted some electron-sized particles that veered the wrong way in a magnetic field. They were uncertain how to interpret the finding, but a few months later, Carl D. Anderson in the

United States did the same experiment and identified the positron, a positively charged electron. For this first discovery of antimatter, Anderson, too, won a Nobel Prize.

Clearly the field of nuclear physics had become much more competitive than in the days when Marie Curie could spend years purifying radium. Undeterred, the Joliot-Curies continued. At a Solvay Conference in Belgium the next year, 1933, they reported that when they placed polonium next to a thin sheet of aluminum, neutrons and positrons emerged. The respected experimentalist Lise Meitner disputed their findings, but Niels Bohr and Wolfgang Pauli privately encouraged them to continue. Back in the laboratory, they made the discovery that when bombarded with alpha particles, the aluminum did emit neutrons. But then, even when the polonium was removed, the aluminum continued to emit particles—this time only positrons. What was happening, they realized, was that when an alpha particle entered the aluminum nucleus, it ejected a neutron and temporarily became a radioactive isotope of phosphorus, which sat two places further along the periodic table. The new radioactive nucleus then emitted a positron and became a stable nucleus of silicon.

On January 15, 1934, Irène and Frédéric demonstrated their experiment to Marie Curie and Paul Langevin. It was a moment laden with significance. Using polonium, a radioactive element discovered by Marie Curie thirty-six years earlier, the Joliot-Curies had succeeded in making a normal element radioactive. To conclude the demonstration, Irène and Frédéric gave Marie a tube containing a sample of the first laboratory-created radioactive isotope. Marie held the tube of radioactive phosphorus to a Geiger counter. Hearing it click, she knew her daughter would win a Nobel Prize. Her Radium Institute would continue to flourish. For the frail Marie, the reassurance came just in time. A few months later, the 67-year-old discoverer of radioactivity died of aplastic anemia, undoubtedly a result of her longtime radiation exposure.

Researchers all over Europe and America quickly recognized the significance of the Joliot-Curies' discovery. Instead of laboring to purify radium or polonium, scien-

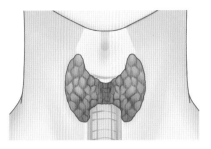

Nuclear medicine *uses unstable isotopes, called radioisotopes, for diagnosis, imaging, and treatment. Radioisotopes are created in a nuclear reactor or cyclotron by adding an extra neutron to an element's nucleus. Once linked to biological compounds, these radioisotopes are injected into a patient's bloodstream. As the radioisotopes decay, they emit gamma rays, which are collected by special cameras. Because different organs absorb different compounds, radioisotopes allow physicians to visualize certain organs. For example, the thyroid gland takes up Iodine-131, while Technetium-99 lights up brain, bone, liver, spleen, kidneys, and lungs. High doses of radioisotopes can be useful for treating disease, as large doses of gamma radiation damage local tissue. Radioactive iodine treatment, for example, is so precise and effective in treating hyperthyroidism and cancer that it has almost eliminated the need for thyroid surgery.*

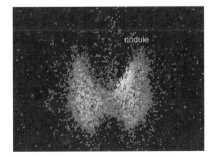

PHYSICS

IRÈNE IN ACADEMIC REGALIA ACCEPTS
AN HONORARY DEGREE FOR HER MOTHER

tists could now bombard much more common metals to create "artificial radiation" as those metals transformed into radioactive isotopes. The discovery allowed research into the structure of the nucleus to leap forward. In 1935, a joint Nobel Prize in Chemistry was awarded to the Joliot-Curies. For their acceptance speech, they shared the podium, with Irène giving the physics portion of their address and Frédéric addressing the chemistry. Nevertheless, articles in the press tended to hail Frédéric as the discoverer and Irène as his able assistant.

After the Nobel Prize, Frédéric was invited to join the faculty of the prestigious Collège de France, where he intended to build an accelerator for particle research. Irène, on the other hand, was invited to join the new anti-fascist Popular Front government as undersecretary of state for scientific research. She accepted the post for three months, calling her service "a sacrifice for the feminist cause in France." Ironically, although she was one of three female ministers, women in France did not win the vote for another nine years.

Irène's blunt nature did not suit her for politics, and when her brief term of service ended, she was happy to return to the lab. However, she found herself increasingly handicapped by bad health. The tuberculosis she had caught during the war required her to take long rest cures in the mountains.

In the late 1930s, after being appointed a professor at the Sorbonne like her mother before her, Irène participated in another competitive scramble toward a Nobel Prize discovery. Enrico Fermi, bombarding uranium with neutrons, thought he had found new elements, which he believed were heavy, "transuranium" elements. Irène Joliot-Curie in Paris and the team of Lise Meitner, Otto Hahn and Fritz Strassman in Berlin raced to replicate the experiments. Irène thought she had found a lanthanum-like element; Hahn scoffed. Then, after Meitner, a Jew, had fled Germany for Sweden, Hahn announced that one of the products was actually barium. Meitner immediately followed up with a manuscript explaining the process of nuclear fission. This time Hahn alone was awarded a Nobel Prize.

Irène was devastated. If only she had still been work-ing with Frédéric, she felt, together they could have cor-rectly interpreted her experiments. Indeed, Frédéric now rushed to join her in further investigations. Joliot and his team worked out equations that predicted the possibility of a chain reaction in uranium. Although they recognized that such a reaction, uncontrolled, could lead to a bomb, they thought such a device could not be completed in time to fight Germany; instead, they focused on designing a nuclear reactor that could supply energy. On October 30, 1939, fearing the consequences if their research fell into German hands, the Joliot-Curies recorded their findings about nuclear reactors on paper, sealed them in an enve-lope, and deposited the envelope at the Academy of Sci-ences, where it remained concealed until 1949. The hidden envelope allowed them to keep their findings secret from the enemy while still claiming scientific priority and credit for them after the war.

As World War II accelerated, Eve Curie left for the United States. She joined the Free French forces under Charles de Gaulle, eventually rising to the rank of lieu-tenant in the women's volunteer medical corps. She also served as a war correspondent in Egypt, Libya, the Soviet Union, and Asia. The Joliot-Curies, on the other hand, decided to join in the struggle while remaining in France. Frédéric arranged for the bulk of France's uranium and heavy water, later used in the Allies' program of nuclear research, to leave the Continent for England. After Paris fell to the Germans in June, 1940, Frédéric joined the Resistance. Despite the presence of Nazi overseers, he managed to use his laboratory at the Collège de France to manufacture both explosives and radio equipment for his comrades. In 1942, after the Gestapo executed some of his friends, including Paul Langevin's son-in-law, Joliot joined the Communist Party, then the most active group in the Resistance.

Irène, meantime, moved in and out of nursing homes and sanatoria, ever more debilitated by tuberculosis. She aged. Shortages of food and continued fevers left her exhausted, and her face became deeply and permanently

Historians estimate that about 400,000 French citizens, or approxi-mately two percent of the adult pop-ulation, actively resisted the German occupation of their country between 1940 and 1945. Small cells of Resis-tance fighters carried out guerrilla warfare and acts of sabotage, but they also published underground newspa-pers, led strikes, gathered intelligence for the Allies, and helped Allied soldiers trapped behind enemy lines to escape. People from all levels of French society and all religions joined the Resistance. About eleven percent of members were women, although they were generally restricted to subordinate roles.

After the Allied landings in Normandy and Provence in 1944, the various Resistance groups organized them-selves into the Free French of the Inte-rior. General Eisenhower, the Supreme Allied Commander in Europe, esti-mated that at the time of the landings the help of the Resistance was worth an extra ten to fifteen Allied divisions.

lined. Still, she did what she could to keep her family strong. In 1944, when Frédéric finally decided to smuggle his family to safety in Switzerland, Irène insisted that they wait until Hélène finished her baccalaureate exams. She and the children escaped across the Alps on D-Day, when the Germans were occupied with the Allied landings in Normandy. Frédéric stayed behind and went underground with the Resistance.

At the end of the war, Missy Meloney, the American journalist, sent Irène streptomycin, a newly discovered antibiotic that finally cured her tuberculosis, though lung damage from years of disease remained. Frédéric was now hailed as a hero and appointed head of the new French Atomic Energy Commission. Soon Irène, too, joined the Commission, where she served for six years. She worked out plans for a large new center for nuclear physics at Orsay, in the southwestern suburbs of Paris. The center would include a synchrocyclotron, a particle accelerator designed to compensate for the effect of relativity as particles reached very high speeds. The Joliot-Curies continued on the Commission until 1951, when a conservative French government and the rise of the Cold War combined to increase public suspicion of anyone with communist ties. First Joliot and then his wife were dismissed from their public posts.

Meanwhile, other honors accumulated for Irène. In 1946, she became director of the Radium Institute, renamed the Curie Institute. She was active in the peace movement and the movement for women's rights, which continued after French women won the vote in 1945. She became an officer of the Legion of Honor and a member of several foreign academies and scientific societies. Three times she applied for membership in the French Academy of Sciences, and three times her candidacy was defeated; each time she publicized the fact that the backward Academy still refused to accept women members.

In 1948, Irène Joliot-Curie journeyed once more to the United States to help raise funds for refugees from Franco's fascist regime in Spain. Because of Irène's links to communism, the immigration authorities at first refused her entry and detained her overnight in a cell at Ellis Island. Irène, waiting, calmly darned her stockings. The French government protested, and the next morning Irène was allowed to enter the country. With her usual bluntness, she told the press that although she wasn't a Communist, "In the United States, they prefer the Fascists and even the Nazis to the Communists. They think that the first and the second have more respect for money."

In the 1950s, Frédéric became increasingly ill with radiation-induced hepatitis. Irène, on the other hand, felt stronger than she had in a long time, and she worked in the laboratory every day. Then, in February 1956, while visiting the family ski chalet in the Alps, she fell suddenly ill and was rushed home by train. When she checked into the Radium Institute's hospital, the doctors diagnosed leukemia. Years of exposure to radiation had caught up with her, as they had with her mother and husband. Calm as ever, Irène told a childhood friend, "I am not afraid of death. I have had such a thrilling life!"

Irène Joliot Curie died on March 17, 1956. She was fifty-eight years old. The government staged a national funeral for her but, at her family's request, omitted military and religious ceremonies. She was survived by her daughter Hélène, who married Paul Langevin's grandson and became a noted nuclear physicist in her own right; her son Pierre, a noted biophysicist; and her husband Frédéric, who died two years after his wife, another victim of what he called "our occupational disease." Indeed, Eve, the only member of the family not to work with radiation, lived on in New York City past the age of one hundred.

Today, partly as a result of the Joliot-Curies' work, France derives over 75 percent of its electrical power from nuclear energy, and radioactive isotopes play an important role in both medical diagnosis and in cancer therapy. The daughter of two great physicists, Irène Joliot-Curie carried on the family tradition and, despite living through two wars and struggling for decades against a devastating disease, made key scientific advances. She remained always dedicated to her faith in science, writing in the last year of her life, "Science is the foundation of all progress that improves human life and diminishes suffering."

PHYSICS

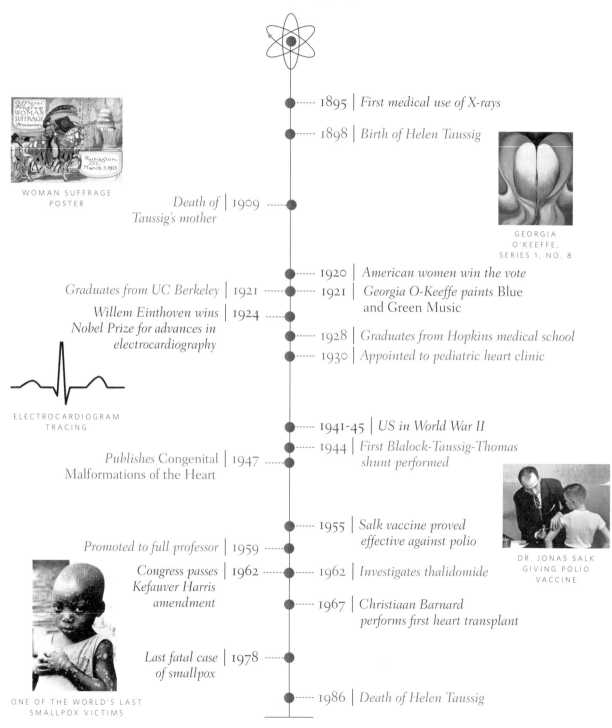

Timeline | 1895-1986

WOMAN SUFFRAGE
POSTER

1895 | First medical use of X-rays

1898 | Birth of Helen Taussig

Death of | 1909
Taussig's mother

GEORGIA
O'KEEFFE,
SERIES 1, NO. 8

1920 | American women win the vote

Graduates from UC Berkeley | 1921 ---- 1921 | Georgia O-Keeffe paints Blue
and Green Music

Willem Einthoven wins | 1924
Nobel Prize for advances in
electrocardiography

1928 | Graduates from Hopkins medical school

1930 | Appointed to pediatric heart clinic

ELECTROCARDIOGRAM
TRACING

1941-45 | US in World War II

1944 | First Blalock-Taussig-Thomas
shunt performed

Publishes Congenital | 1947
Malformations of the Heart

1955 | Salk vaccine proved
effective against polio

Promoted to full professor | 1959

Congress passes | 1962 ---- 1962 | Investigates thalidomide
Kefauver Harris
amendment

DR. JONAS SALK
GIVING POLIO
VACCINE

1967 | Christiaan Barnard
performs first heart transplant

Last fatal case | 1978
of smallpox

1986 | Death of Helen Taussig

ONE OF THE WORLD'S LAST
SMALLPOX VICTIMS

11 | *Saving Blue Babies*

Helen Taussig

1898-1986 | *United States*

Before Dr. Helen Taussig found a solution in the 1940s, about a thousand American children died each year from complications of an inborn heart abnormality known as Tetralogy of Fallot, the most common cause of "blue baby syndrome." Blood flowing through the babies' bodies did not carry enough oxygen to give it the bright red color we expect in arterial blood. Instead, darkened, oxygen-poor blood lent a bluish cast to the babies' lips and fingers.

One of the heart's main functions is to pump oxygen through the body so it can be used by muscles, the brain, and other organs. In the normal heart, venous blood, depleted of oxygen, returns through the right atrium to the right ventricle. The right ventricle pumps the blood through the lungs, in a journey known as the pulmonary circulation. In the lungs, the blood absorbs oxygen before returning through the left atrium to the muscular left ventricle. Finally, the left ventricle pumps the oxygenated blood, against high pressure, out through the aorta to all the arteries of the body, forming the systemic circulation.

In the congenital condition known as Tetralogy of Fallot, four abnormalities combine to cause mixing of the pulmonary and systemic circulation. The pulmonary artery leading from the right ventricle to the lungs is small or partially blocked. A ventricular septal defect or hole between the ventricles allows some venous blood in the right ventricle to bypass the lungs and instead pass through the hole and out through an enlarged aorta to the body. As a result, the oxygen level of the arterial blood is chronically low. Children with Tetralogy of Fallot are blue and breathless, so easily winded that they have to squat frequently to catch their breath. At times, so little oxygen reaches their brains that they faint or lapse into longer periods of unconsciousness. In the 1940s, many children with this defect died as babies, and most of the rest died in childhood.

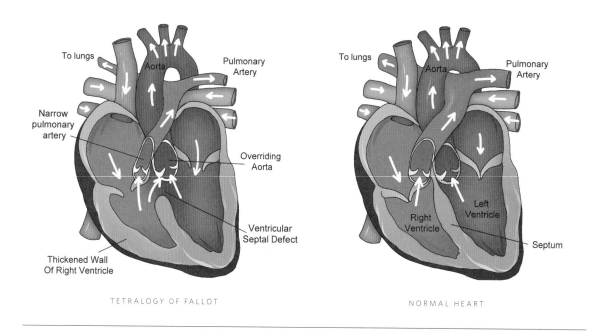

TETRALOGY OF FALLOT   NORMAL HEART

Helen Taussig, born in 1898, was the daughter of a prominent Harvard economics professor and a mother who had studied botany and biology at the Radcliffe Annex before it became Radcliffe College. She grew up surrounded by good books, music, and learned conversation. Still, although she appeared intelligent and curious, she struggled in school. Reading was such an ordeal for her that when called upon to read aloud before the class, she perspired, felt nauseated, and sometimes broke into tears. Once she even ran away from school. Helen's teachers couldn't understand her behavior. She had every advantage at home, and her three older siblings thrived in their classes. The girl's difficulties with reading, Helen's teachers concluded, must be for lack of effort. So they scolded and shamed her, trying to motivate her to try harder.

Helen Taussig had the misfortune to suffer from dyslexia before it was named or understood. Dyslexia is a disorder of the brain that makes learning to read difficult in spite of good instruction and normal intelligence. For a dyslexic person, letters reverse themselves on the page, or words twist themselves into unintelligible scribbles. No amount of scolding or shaming solves the problem. Luckily for Helen Taussig, her professor father remained always calm and encouraging despite her difficulties, reading with her for hours and urging her not to give up. Although she failed spelling and reading many times in elementary school, Helen persevered.

When Helen Taussig was nine years old, her mother fell ill with tuberculosis. The family hired a housekeeper and nursemaid to help with family chores, and they installed an elevator that the children could operate to help their mother get up and down stairs. Despite healthy food, fresh air, and rest, which were the mainstays of treatment at the time, Edith Guild Taussig's strength gradually declined, and she died when Helen was eleven.

Near the time of her mother's death, Helen herself was diagnosed with a "mild tubercular condition." Especially during summers on Cape Cod, she slept outdoors on the porch to get more fresh air, and once fall came she attended school for only a few hours in the morning. Her father helped her with additional lessons at home.

Eventually, Helen did learn to read, as well as to write clearly, although neither ever came easily to her. Her health also improved, and she became an excellent tennis player. By the end of her high school years at the private Cambridge School for Girls, she had achieved mostly As and Bs, and her headmistress wrote in a letter of recommendation, "[Helen Taussig] has an excellent mind, good habits of study, is faithful and conscientious. Her attitude toward her companions and teachers is cheerful and courteous and she takes first rank in her class . . . Her womanly qualities are marked and easily recognized."

Taussig was admitted to Radcliffe College, near her Cambridge home. She struggled academically her first semester but soon improved

PROFESSOR FRANK WILLIAM TAUSSIG, HELEN'S FATHER

her grades. Tall and somewhat gawky, she played tennis and basketball and took on the role of footman in a play. But she chafed at being so close to home. After two years, she transferred to the University of California at Berkeley. At Berkeley she had a chance to "stand on my own two feet," away from the influence and reputation of her professor father. There she continued her tennis and theater. She hiked in Yosemite in winter, she advised younger students, and she graduated in 1921. Then she returned to Cambridge to think about a career.

Taussig's paternal grandfather had been a Civil War and country doctor, and Taussig thought medicine might suit her. Her father advised her to consider public health, which he pronounced a more suitable career for a woman, so Taussig presented herself to the dean of the new Harvard School of Public Health for an interview. He told her that to enter the school, she would first have to study for two years at the medical school. Only then would she be permitted to take two years of courses in public health. As a woman, though, she would not be admitted as a degree candidate. Taussig was incredulous. "Who wants to study for four years and get no degree for all that work?" she demanded. The smiling dean replied, "No one, I hope."

Despite this clear signal that she was unwelcome, Taussig did begin to take medical school classes at Harvard. Although Harvard Medical School did not admit women as degree candidates until 1945, it did allow women to sit in on some classes, so long as they did not "contaminate"

YOUNG HELEN TAUSSIG

the men. In histology class, where young men studied the microscopic anatomy of human tissues, Taussig had to sit far in the back of the lecture hall. To examine slides through the microscope she was actually required to sit in a separate room altogether. Still, she did well enough that her instructor advised her to continue her anatomy studies at nearby Boston University, where at least she would receive credit for her work.

At Boston University, Taussig found a mentor in Dr. Alexander Begg, an anatomy professor who urged her to study muscle bundles of the heart. "It won't do you any harm to get interested in one of the larger organs of the body," he told Taussig. After months of experiments, she showed that strips of tissue from an ox heart could be made to beat rhythmically in solution, the first time this had been demonstrated with mammalian tissue. When she got the conditions just right, she made the experiment work not just with ox hearts, but also with heart tissue from pigs, dogs, rabbits, sheep, and even a human. With Begg, Taussig published her first scientific paper, "Rhythmic Contractions in Isolated Strips of Mammalian Ventricles" in 1925. As they worked together on the paper, Begg told her she really ought to apply to a medical school that would admit women. In 1924, Helen Taussig entered the Johns Hopkins School of Medicine, where she would stay for the next sixty years.

At Hopkins, Taussig continued to do research on the heart while taking classes. On top of her dyslexia she faced a new challenge, a gradual decline in her hearing that seemed to date from a childhood case of whooping cough. She sat near the front of the lecture hall, straining to catch the lecturer's words, and she taught herself to lip read as well as she could. On graduating, she applied for an internship position that was to be offered to only one woman. While waiting to hear if she would get the post, she worked in the heart clinic.

In the end, another woman got the adult medicine internship Taussig had wanted. Disappointed, she went on to complete two years of an internship in pediatrics instead. In 1930, because of her dual expertise in hearts and children, she was appointed a faculty member in the new pediatric cardiology clinic. By this time her hearing had declined even further. She wore a large locket-like hearing aid under her dress and used a special amplifying stethoscope to listen to the hearts of her patients. Most of all, though, she learned to gain a great deal of information through touch. By placing her fingertips lightly on a baby's chest wall she could feel the rumble of pressured blood flow that others heard as a heart murmur.

Many of the patients Taussig saw at the Harriet Lane Home for Invalid Children at Hopkins suffered from rheumatic heart disease. These were children who developed rheumatic fever following a streptococcal infection. In a late reaction to the infection, the sufferer's immune system attacked the body's own heart valves, leaving them scarred and thickened. Children developed heart murmurs and eventually abnormal blood flow. Today, rheumatic fever is prevented by giving penicillin to children with strep infection, and old rheumatic heart disease can be treated with open-heart surgery to replace the damaged valves.

Aside from children with rheumatic heart disease, Taussig became the primary care provider for a number of cyanotic (blue) children, those with congenital malformations of the heart. She later remembered, "[Other doctors] gladly referred their 'blue babies' to me, because nothing could be done for them." Taussig used a new imaging technique, fluoroscopy, which takes moving X-ray pictures of a patient placed between the X-ray machine and a fluorescent screen. Taussig turned the patients so she could see the outline of the heart from all directions. She learned to put together information from the moving shadow of the heart, her sense of touch and limited hearing, and her knowledge of heart anatomy from dissections and autopsies, to determine the fault in the plumbing of her blue babies' hearts. But the painful fact remained that, besides her gentle examinations and advice to the parents, she had no treatment to offer her young patients.

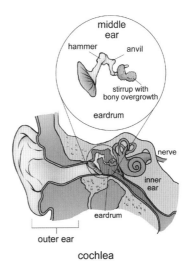

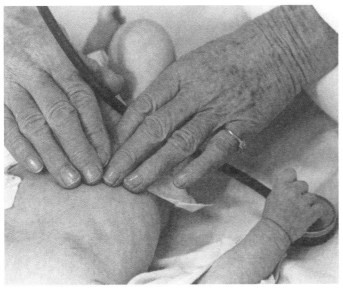

HANDS OF HELEN TAUSSIG

Helen Taussig suffered from **otosclerosis**, *which is a common cause of hearing loss in young or middle-aged adults. In normal hearing, sound waves entering the outer ear cause the thin membrane of the eardrum to vibrate. Three tiny bones of the middle ear, the hammer, anvil, and stirrup, then amplify the sound vibrations and transmit them to the fluid-filled cochlea, a spiral structure in the inner ear. Waves in the cochlear fluid activate hair cells, creating an electrical signal that travels along the auditory nerve to be heard as sound.*

In otosclerosis, abnormal bony growth locks one of the middle ear bones, usually the stirrup, in place. Hearing loss comes on gradually. Although a hearing aid can amplify sound, surgery to bypass the abnormal bone may be required.

Over time, Taussig noticed that while most blue babies seemed to turn suddenly worse a few days after birth, others did well for the first few months before taking a sudden nosedive. The cause, she reasoned, lay in a fetal blood vessel called the ductus arteriosus. This blood vessel attaches the aorta to the pulmonary artery in the fetus, and it normally closes down as the lungs inflate shortly after birth. In some of the blue babies, the ductus arteriosus stayed open for several months, shunting additional blood through the lungs and improving the overall level of oxygen in the babies' blood. If only a way could be found to keep the shunt open, the blue babies might live longer. She talked to Dr. Robert Gross at Boston Children's Hospital about her idea, but got nowhere. Taussig later said, "It seemed pretty foolish to him to have me suggest that he put the ductus in again. I think he thought it was [one] of the craziest things he'd heard in a long time. So

VIVIEN THOMAS

I went back to Baltimore and waited. When I heard Dr. Alfred Blalock was coming to Baltimore, I thought this was my chance."

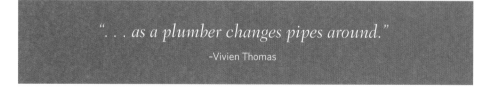

". . . as a plumber changes pipes around."
-Vivien Thomas

In 1943, Taussig approached Alfred Blalock, the new chief of surgery at Hopkins, to discuss the problem with him. Blalock invited his surgical technician, Vivien Thomas, into the conversation. Thomas, a skilled experimenter who often operated on dogs, was an African American man whose formal education had not extended beyond high school. Thomas remembered Taussig as tall and slim with a strong New England accent. Taussig carefully explained Tetralogy of Fallot, demonstrating it with a collection of hearts from the medical school's pathological collection. Then she posed her challenge: Could the surgeons create a new connection between the pulmonary and systemic circulation "as a plumber changes pipes around" to reproduce the effect of the ductus arteriosus?

Intrigued, Blalock and Thomas went to work. Their plan was to create a connection between the subclavian artery and the pulmonary artery. First, though, Thomas did the operation hundreds of times in dogs. His first success was in a dog named Anna, who survived six years after the surgery, and whose portrait eventually hung in a pediatrics ward at Hopkins.

In November 1944, the team decided it was time to try the operation on a human patient. Dr. Blalock scheduled time in the laboratory to practice with Thomas, but before he had time to do more than assist on one dog operation, a human patient, fifteen-month-old Eileen Saxon, began to deteriorate rapidly. Again and again she started to pant for breath and then lost consciousness. Desperately ill, the little girl was wheeled into the operating room on November 29th. Taussig stood beside the anesthesiologist at the patient's head, while Thomas stood on a stool at Blalock's shoulder, giving him technical advice and answering questions. The little girl survived the operation, and despite a rocky hospital course, she went home after two months. Unfortunately, she died during another operation a few months later. Still, based on this partial success, the team operated on two more children, one of them a nine-year-old boy, in February of the next year.

In April, Blalock and Taussig wrote a paper called "The Surgical Treatment of Malformations of the Heart" describing the procedure, which quickly became known as the Blalock-Taussig shunt or sometimes the Blalock-Thomas-Taussig procedure. The paper led to a blizzard of interest. Parents from all over the country and even abroad brought their cyanotic children to the cardiac clinic. Carefully and efficiently, Taussig examined the children, determining which could benefit from the surgery and which, because of other complicating defects, could not. Thomas remembered Taussig as always calm and much more cheerful now that she had help to offer the children. Meanwhile, visiting surgeons crowded in to observe the operation in room 706, now known as the "heart room."

Taussig felt personally responsible for all the blue babies who came under her care. What Blalock's cardiac resident Denton Cooley called Taussig's "fiercely protective, mother-hen-like approach to her young patients" sometimes drove Blalock to distraction, and he tasked Cooley with keeping "Taussig and her women"—mostly postgraduate fellows in pediatric cardiology—away from him. Cooley welcomed the opportunity to spend more time with Taussig, learning from her as both a researcher and a clinical doctor.

Taussig kept in touch with the more than one thousand children that she eventually referred for the surgery. She corresponded with them, and many years later she published a twenty-eight year follow-up study on all the blue babies operated on at Hopkins in the first six years. Contrary to the fears of critics, these children grew up healthy and often quite accomplished, showing no signs as a group of being intellectually disabled due to an early shortage of oxygen delivered to the brain.

In 1947, Taussig published a textbook titled *Congenital Malformations of the Heart*, based almost wholly on her own experience and examination of patients. The book established pediatric cardiology as an independent specialty, and Taussig eventually trained 123 other doctors in the new field. These doctors referred to themselves as the Loyal Knights of Taussig. Of being a teacher, Taussig wrote, "We strive to teach our students all we know, and we expect them to get ahead of us and further advance knowledge. We take pride in their achievements, but we all strive to stay ahead of them as long as we possibly can . . ." She also gave lectures. Because her deafness sometimes

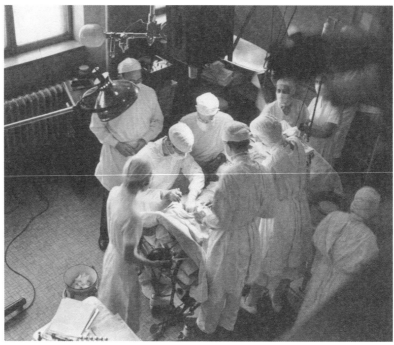

SURGERY ON A "BLUE BABY."
NOTE THOMAS STANDING BEHIND BLALOCK

made her voice become high and piercing when she tried to project, she stationed one of her cardiac fellows at the back of the lecture hall to signal to her when she needed to lower her pitch.

Devoted as she was to her work, Taussig also enjoyed time away. She spent several weeks each summer on Cape Cod, writing in the mornings and relaxing with swims and walks on the beach in the afternoons and evenings. Guests were welcome as long as they respected the schedule and took care of their own breakfast. She also loved to garden and to travel abroad. In 1958 she led a delegation of six women doctors on an exchange program to the Soviet Union. On the lawn of her lakeside home, Taussig held an annual pediatric cardiology picnic during which researchers exchanged insights as they dined on crab cakes and macaroni with tomatoes.

> *"Whatever field you choose, just work quietly and steadily to make this world a better place, and your life will be worthwhile."*

Although Taussig received twenty honorary degrees and international acclaim for her work, she still experienced barriers and discrimination as a woman. Blalock was elected to the National Academy of Sciences in 1947; Taussig waited twenty-seven more years for her election. Blalock was made full professor at Hopkins when he first arrived in 1941. In 1946, Taussig, who had led the pediatric cardiology clinic for sixteen years, was promoted from assistant to associate professor. Only in 1959, shortly before retirement, was she finally made a full professor. "Promotion was slow and the men didn't too readily share their medical experience with the women," she wrote, though the chief of pediatrics "was generous to women and tried to make me see that the quality of our work was what was important." To younger women, she counseled patience: "If your work is good enough, men will respect you and will grant you what is due you. Whatever field you choose, just work quietly and steadily to make this world a better place, and your life will be worthwhile." She trained both men and women doctors and hired black staff members for the clinic at a time when even the operating rooms at Hopkins were segregated by race.

At a dinner in January 1962, Taussig heard from one of her trainees, a German pediatrician named Dr. Alois Beuren, about a disturbing increase in a certain kind of birth deformity in Europe. The condition was called "phocomelia," or "seal limbs." Children born with the deformity had short arms and sometimes legs, and they often lacked well-formed hands and feet. The number of babies born with phocomelia had been rising sharply, and no one knew why. The disease did not seem to run in families. Radiation, viral infection, and pollution were all raised as possible causes, but others thought the cause could be a sleeping pill called thalidomide. Originally sold in Germany as a sedative, thalidomide quickly became popular as a treatment for the morning sickness of early pregnancy.

Almost immediately, Taussig realized the importance of the issue. No one had established the potential for a drug taken by a mother to cause abnormalities in her unborn child. In fact, doctors believed that the placenta was an effective barrier that would prevent drugs taken by the mother from reaching the fetal circulation. If thalidomide were really causing phocomelia, not only must it be kept out of the United States, the whole method for approving new drugs for pregnant women needed to change.

Taussig requested a leave from Hopkins and flew to Germany to learn more. One of the most financially

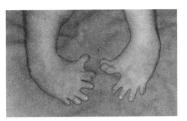

FEET OF A BABY WHOSE MOTHER HAD TAKEN THALIDOMIDE DURING PREGNANCY

Until the twentieth century, Americans had little protection against quack medicines or unsafe food products. However, in 1906, President Theodore Roosevelt signed the Wiley Act, outlawing the interstate transport of "adulterated" food or drugs. The Department of Agriculture's Bureau of Chemistry was given responsibility for examining food and drugs.

By the 1930s, journalists were highlighting stark failures of the regulatory system, pointing to radioactive drinks, a mascara that caused blindness, and worthless quack "cures" for diabetes and tuberculosis. In response, President Franklin D. Roosevelt signed the new Food, Drug, and Cosmetic Act in 1938. The act required that all drugs undergo review before entering the market. In the 1950s, a requirement was added stating that consumers could buy certain drugs only with a prescription.

After the U.S. barely missed the thalidomide tragedy that struck Europe in the 1950s, the new Kefauver-Harris Amendment required drug manufacturers to show new medicines to be effective as well as safe. FDA approval is now a prolonged and rigorous process, although occasional drugs still need to be recalled after they are on the market when serious side effects occur.

successful drugs developed up to that time, thalidomide was already being marketed in forty-six countries under more than thirty different trade names. In the United States, it was being used on a test basis while awaiting approval from the Food and Drug Administration. At the FDA, one steadfast reviewer, a woman MD/PhD named Frances Oldham Kelsey, was resisting pressure to approve the drug, demanding that the manufacturer complete more testing first.

"A mild and supposedly safe sedative . . ."

What Taussig saw in Germany convinced her of the drug's dangers. On her return, she reported to her colleagues at Hopkins and then at a special session of an American College of Physicians conference. She told them that a "mild and supposedly safe sedative taken by pregnant women has deformed the limbs and other organs of several thousand infants in West Germany, England, Canada, and other countries." Taussig published her concerns in *Scientific American* and the *Journal of the American Medical Association*, and as an editorial in *Science*. Newspapers blared warnings. President Kennedy addressed the problem in a press conference, and the FDA, rather than approving the drug, worked to inform every medical practitioner in the country of its dangers.

HELEN TAUSSIG, FROM THE COVER OF *MODERN MEDICINE*, 1963

As a result, although more than 10,000 infants with phocomelia were born worldwide, only seventeen cases occurred in the United States. Together, two brave and outspoken women had averted a catastrophe. In 1962, Congress unanimously passed the Kefauver-Harris Amendment to strengthen drug regulation and prevent similar crises in the future.

Taussig formally retired from Johns Hopkins in 1963. She stopped attending the clinic, but continued to lecture, teach, and write papers. She advocated in favor of animal research, hospice care, and legalized abortion, especially in the case of suspected birth defects. In 1964, President Lyndon Johnson awarded her the Presidential Medal of Freedom, and in 1965 she became the first female president of the American Heart Association. In the 1960s, she also had an operation that restored much of her hearing. At the age of 78, she moved to a retirement community in Pennsylvania, but she continued to make trips to the Delaware Museum of Natural History and the library at the College of

Physicians of Philadelphia to do background research. In all, she published 41 papers during her retirement. She also remained socially active, inviting friends for summers at the Cape, sleeping in the fresh air, and swimming throughout the summer months.

In February 1986, the concert pianist Samuel Sanders, one of Helen Taussig's blue babies, gave a special recital in honor of the 87-year-old cardiologist at the Peabody Conservatory of Music, which is associated with Johns Hopkins. At the Baltimore hotel where she stayed that night, Taussig was greeted by the bellhop, another former patient.

A few months later, on May 20, 1986, Helen Taussig was driving a carful of friends to vote in a local election when she pulled out in front of another car. The resulting collision killed her before paramedics arrived. In 2005, Johns Hopkins established four colleges in its School of Medicine to give students a stronger sense of identity and connection. Three of the colleges are named after Frances Sabin, Vivien Thomas, and Helen Taussig.

Timeline | 1897-1979

ILLUSTRATIONS FROM WAR OF THE WORLDS BY H.G.WELLS

HG Wells writes | 1897
The War of the Worlds *about a Martian invasion*

1900 | Birth of Cecilia Payne

1904 | Cecilia's father dies

Family moves to London | 1912

World War I | 1914-1918

1912 | Henrietta Leavitt discovers period/ brightness relationship in variable stars

1920 | Edwin Hubble demonstrates more galaxies beyond the Milky Way

Graduates from Cambridge and goes to | 1923 work at Harvard Observatory

1925 | Proposes that stars are composed mostly of hydrogen and helium; receives PhD

Charles Lindbergh | 1927 flies across the Atlantic

1934 | Marries Sergei Gaposchkin.

Fritz Zwicky | 1937 discovers dark matter

1940 | First Bugs Bunny cartoon

CHARLES LINDBERGH WITH THE SPIRIT OF ST. LOUIS

1942-1945 | US in World War II

BUGS BUNNY

Publishes four books on astronomy | 1954-1957

1956 | Becomes full professor and chair of astronomy at Harvard

GALAXY

1968 | Stanley Kubrick releases 2001: A Space Odyssey

MUSIC ALBUM FROM 2001: A SPACE ODYSSEY

1979 | Death of Cecilia Payne-Gaposchkin

12 | *What the Stars Are Made Of*

Cecilia Payne-Gaposchkin
1900-1979 | *England and United States*

BEE ORCHID

In the long grass of the apple orchard stood a flower with light purple petals. Nestled at their center rested a brown and yellow, slightly furred blob that resembled a bumblebee. Cecilia Payne, eight years old, had never before seen a bee orchid, but she recognized it at once from descriptions she had heard, and her heart leapt. She ran to tell her mother, who had the gardener transplant the flower to a spot under a spruce tree. There Cecilia created a little shrine and vowed to dedicate herself to the study of nature. Other experiences confirmed her resolve: a meteor, Halley's Comet, and the Daylight Comet of 1910. Cecilia decided to become a scientist. Her only worry was that everything would be found out before she was old enough to make discoveries of her own.

Cecilia Payne grew up surrounded by women. Her beloved father, a lawyer and gifted musician, died when she was four years old.

CECILIA

She had aunts, great-aunts, and step-great-aunts, most of them unmarried. They included a pianist, a painter, and a botanist. Still, even at a young age, Cecilia understood that to be female was a disadvantage: when her brother Humfry was born, she found that suddenly he "was the one who really mattered."

When Cecilia was six years old, a girls' school opened across the street. Attending until age twelve, the pupils learned French and German, algebra and geometry, and measurement. They memorized poetry and a smattering of Latin. Forced to use her right hand although she was left-handed, Cecilia became ambidextrous but also picked up a lifelong confusion in distinguishing left from right. School delighted Cecilia, and home was rich both in music and books in many languages. Gifted with perfect pitch, Cecilia played piano and violin.

When Cecilia was twelve, the family moved to London so that Humfry could prepare for an elite school. Cecilia was enrolled at a Church of England school that emphasized the classics, setting her back two years in mathematics—"Alas for my beloved quadratic equations!" she later wrote—and made little time for science. Skeptical about prayer, Cecilia tried an experiment: she prayed for good marks in one exam and not another. The results did not match the prayer, and although later she admitted that perhaps the test had not been a fair one, Cecilia made up her mind that "the only legitimate request to God is for courage." She began to write reams of verse, including a blank verse tragedy of a scientist who compromises his integrity in pursuit of money.

In Cecilia's second year at the new school, a Miss Dalglish arrived to teach science. Miss Dalglish taught botany and chemistry, and Cecilia adored her. The devoted pupil spent hours drawing botanical specimens, and in the tiny lab at the top of the school she contemplated the chemical elements with a kind of awe. When Cecilia was awarded a book prize at the end of the year, instead of selecting Shakespeare or Milton as expected, she insisted upon receiving a textbook on fungi.

Then Miss Dalglish left, and school became lonelier. Noting an adolescent growth of hair on her face, Cecilia went to a doctor who told her nothing could be done about it. "Never mind, Cecilia," he told her. "You've got brains. Make something of them." Tall, broad-shouldered, and convinced she was unattractive, Cecilia withdrew into shyness. But she insisted that she wanted to pursue science, which meant studying German and advanced mathematics, neither of which her school offered. The principal, a religious woman, told Cecilia sternly that she was "prostituting her gifts" by choosing science, and that the school could do no more for her.

At seventeen, Cecilia moved to the St. Paul's School for Girls, where to her delight she could immerse herself in chemistry and physics. There was also a music master, Gustav Holst, perhaps best known as composer of *The Planets*, who praised her violin playing and told her she should become a musician. At the same time, Cecilia and her younger brother and sister reveled in the theater and opera of London, and whenever they could they staged plays for younger children in the local church hall.

The dream of becoming a scientist could never have come true if Cecilia had not won a full scholarship to Newnham College at Cambridge. The college was primarily a residence hall; the girls took courses with Cambridge men, although graduates received certificates instead of Cambridge degrees. Payne enrolled in the course of Natural Sciences, intending to become a botanist, while taking coursework in physics and chemistry as well. The only young woman in Ernest Rutherford's physics lecture, she was required to sit alone in the front row. One of her chemistry lab instructors shouted at women for disturbing the magnetic equipment with their steel-stiffened corsets.

One day Payne attended a lecture by the astronomer and physicist Arthur Eddington, who had recently returned from a scientific expedition to observe a solar eclipse in Brazil. The eclipse had allowed Eddington to confirm Einstein's prediction that light would bend around a massive object like the sun. Eddington's lecture on astronomy and relativity struck Payne like a "thunderclap;" she went home and wrote the lecture down, as she later testified, "word for word." The next day she informed her tutors that she wished to change her subject to astronomy.

SIR ARTHUR EDDINGTON

At Cambridge at the time, astronomy was considered a branch of mathematics, and since it was too late to change her course of study entirely, instead Payne concentrated in physics. Though she attended physics labs and lectures, she spent more and more of her time on astronomy. On the campus of Newnham College she fixed up an abandoned observatory and gave demonstrations to the public. She attended astronomy lectures wherever she could find them, and she convinced Eddington to assign her a couple of research projects. Still, she knew England had no place for a female astronomer. Her friend A.J. Comrie, a PhD in astronomy who had lost both a leg and his hearing in World War I, advised her that America might be different. He escorted her to London to hear a lecture on globular clusters by Harlow Shapley, the young new director of the Harvard Observatory. Once again, Payne found herself mesmerized. After the lecture she told Shapley she would like to come work with him, and he said he would be delighted. A few months later, armed with her Cambridge degree and a fellowship, Cecilia Payne sailed for America.

PICKERING'S HAREM

Founded in 1839, the Harvard College Observatory had built a reputation through the photography and careful cataloguing of stars. Much of the work of stellar classification had been done by a series of underpaid and largely unrecognized women known as computers, or sometimes as "Pickering's Harem." These included Annie Jump Cannon, who did invaluable work in stellar classification, and Henrietta Leavitt, who discovered the relationship between the brightness of variable stars and their period of variation. Like his predecessor at the Observatory, the charismatic new director, Shapley, tended to measure the magnitude of planned projects in projected "woman-years."

Because, unlike the computers, she came with a fellowship, Payne was able to choose her own project. She decided to study stellar atmospheres, using spectroscopy and her knowledge of quantum physics to determine their composition. Shapley wanted her to write a PhD thesis. Since Harvard had no department of astronomy, Shapley thought Payne should be admitted to the physics department. However, the physics chairman, Theodore Lyman, was determined never to admit a woman, so in the end, Shapley created a graduate school of astronomy with occasional lectures and Payne as its first, and at the time, only student. By the time she received her PhD two years later, she had already published six papers. In her papers and her thesis, Payne laid out her discovery that elements in stars were remarkably uniform, with variations in their spectra due mostly to differences in temperature. Moreover, stellar atmospheres consisted primarily of helium and hydrogen rather than the nitrogen, oxygen, silicon, and iron so abundant on earth.

Payne's discovery upended conventional wisdom about what elements made up the universe. Shapley and others expected the stars to be similar to the earth in makeup, but Payne's spectra showed otherwise. Otto Struve, a leading astronomer, later declared Payne's work to be "undoubtedly the most brilliant PhD thesis ever written in astronomy." By bringing her knowledge of quantum physics to bear on the problem of stellar atmospheres, she had helped establish the field of astrophysics. A clear and witty writer herself, Payne valued elegant scientific writing. She stated, "Good scientific thought has an esthetic perfection, which reveals itself in the language of presentation," and she lamented how certain scientists resisted her attempts to make their writing clearer. At the same time, Payne's conclusions on helium and hydrogen contradicted the beliefs of her thesis advisor, Henry Norris Russell of Princeton. At Russell's urging, Payne qualified her findings, writing that the abundance of the two lightest elements was "improbably high and . . . almost certainly not real." A few years later, Russell confirmed Payne's conjecture, and the idea of helium and hydrogen abundance became widely accepted, forming the foundation for an eventual understanding of the nuclear fusion that powers stars. Although in his own work Russell briefly credited Cecilia Payne, the scientific community generally credited Russell, not Payne, with the discovery that the sun was composed of a different mix of elements than the earth.

> *"I had given in to Authority when I believed it was right . . ."*

With the end of her PhD research, and after publishing her monograph *Stellar Atmospheres*, Payne came to the end of her fellowship. Shapley asked her to stay, and though the job came with little money and a loss of freedom to choose her own work, Payne accepted. She had to pawn her violin and jewelry to fill the gap between her last fellowship check and first paycheck. Shapley asked her to continue Henrietta Leavitt's work on photometry, measuring the intensity of light from different stars. The work was demanding and at times tedious. Payne concluded that some of the light from stars was being absorbed by interstellar matter. Once again, Shapley and Russell

disagreed with her, and this time she did not publish her findings. Later, after Struve demonstrated the absorption effect, Payne wrote, "I was to blame for not having pressed my point. I had given in to Authority when I believed I was right." Ensconced in the atmosphere of the Observatory, where women observed but men built theories, she had allowed herself to be intimidated intellectually.

Soon Shapley set Payne to work cataloging variable stars. He also assigned her to be the editor of the Observatory publications. She loved the hurry of publishing, the smell of freshly printed paper, the detailed work of proofreading, the art of creating diagrams, and the craft of layout. Editing called on skills honed during her classical education, and no doubt the careful reading of manuscripts kept her abreast of current astronomy. She also became convinced that muddled or inelegant writing revealed muddled thinking. At the same time she grew so tired of conflicts over priority and claims to be first author that she wrote, "I have come to wish

ANNIE JUMP CANNON 1922

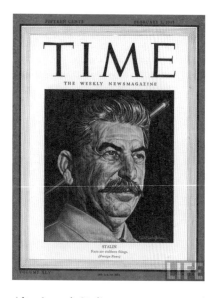

*After **Joseph Stalin** came to power in the Soviet Union in 1924, he clamped down on the arts and sciences. In biology, Stalin promoted a quack agriculturalist named Lysenko, who denied Darwinian evolution and claimed that crops could be "trained" to grow in winter. Lysenko's manipulation of data devastated Soviet agriculture and contributed to widespread starvation, but scientists who spoke out against him were imprisoned or killed.*

In physics, the Soviet authorities condemned quantum mechanics and relativity, and in statistics they denied the law of large numbers and the idea of random deviation.

In 1936 and 1937, the Soviets purged twenty-nine astronomers, or close to twenty percent of all the astronomers in the Soviet Union. Authorities charged them with bending to foreign science and counter-revolutionary tendencies. The arrested scientists received long prison sentences, and many were executed, among them Cecilia Payne's friend Boris Gerasimovich.

that all scientific work could be published anonymously, to stand or fall by its intrinsic worth."

During the twenties, Payne lectured in astronomy, but as a woman she was never listed in the Harvard catalog. Although she interacted with visiting astronomers from all over the world, she was excluded from Harvard social events and complained that she met fewer Harvard faculty than did the wives of her colleagues. In 1930, as she considered a move to Barnard College, Shapley abruptly raised her salary to $2700, still below the $3000 salary of starting Harvard lecturers in astronomy. He also approved a summer of travel in which Payne visited other American observatories and interacted with astronomers. In 1931, with Shapley's nomination, Payne was finally elected to the Harvard faculty club. Gradually, more doors opened.

In 1932 and 1933, a series of events, including the sudden deaths of three friends and an unrequited love affair, created a personal crisis for Cecilia Payne. For years her work, some cooking and knitting, and a few close friendships had been enough for her, but now she resolved, as she put it, to open herself to the world. She took a voyage to Europe and ultimately to Russia to visit the astronomer, Boris Gerasimovich. During two weeks in Russia she experienced the grey, foreboding tension of life under Stalin. One woman took her out to the middle of a turnip field and begged her in tears to find her a job in the States, something Payne had no power to do. Upon leaving Russia, Payne traveled to Germany, where in Berlin and Göttingen she felt the same sense of rising tension. Under the Nazis, as under Stalin, political purity mattered more than scientific merit. More than ever she was grateful for her post in America. Then, at a lecture, she met a Russian astronomer named Sergei Gaposchkin who needed to get out of Germany. Here was someone she could actually help. As soon as Payne was breathing freely again on American shores, she pulled strings to get Gaposchkin a Harvard position, and then traveled to New York to get him a visa. Gaposchkin arrived at

Harvard in November 1933. Three months later, he and Cecilia Payne were married.

Marriage appears to have suited Payne, now Payne-Gaposchkin, better than she had expected. "I had once pictured myself as a rebel against the feminine role," she wrote, "but in this I was wrong. My rebellion was against being thought, and treated, as inferior." Cecilia and Sergei eventually had three children with whom they read books, traveled, played bridge, and held intellectual dinnertime conversation. Payne-Gaposchkin loved to cook with a multitude of spices, leaving Sergei to do the cleaning up. She was a warm mother who managed to discipline her children sufficiently just by giving them looks, or by slapping her hands on the table and crying, "I want silence, and very little of that!" Although they were always frugal, during the years of World War II the Gaposchkins bought a farm in northern Massachusetts, hoping to house a refugee family and also to contribute to the food supply. The first never happened, so the family worked together on the farm, raising chickens, turkeys, two pigs, a cow, a sheep, and a horse. Sergei built a one-room cabin, and Cecilia did the cooking on a tiny wood stove.

At the Observatory, Sergei and Cecilia worked together on variable stars, with Sergei focusing on eclipsing stars. Using the Harvard photographic plates and working with a team, they cataloged two thousand variable stars, recording the periods between their maximum and minimum brightness. Along the way they discovered a number of recurring supernovae.

In the 1940s, the Gaposchkins created a Forum for International Problems, a program of lectures and discussions at the Observatory. Payne-Gaposchkin chaired the program until the discussions among visitors became too heated for promoting peace, at which point she handed it off to other forum members. During the war years she traveled often to lecture and teach, as her career was more developed than her husband's. When the war ended the family traveled extensively in the American West and in Europe.

THE CONSTELLATION CASSIOPEIA CONTAINS A DOUBLE STAR AND TWO BRIGHT VARIABLE STARS.

Variable stars *change in brightness. They fade and then grow brighter in a predictable cycle that may last part of a second or many years. The outer layers of pulsating variable stars swell and shrink. Eclipsing stars are binary stars where one star seems to dim as the other, less luminous star passes in front of it. And some variable stars are actually close binary stars that exchange mass as one draws the atmosphere away from the other. There are even recurring novae, white dwarfs that draw mass from a nearby star and explode as novae several times with many years between explosions. There are now over 150,000 variable stars known, and amateur astronomers have an important role to play in helping to observe their behavior.*

"I find myself cast in the unlikely role of a thin wedge."

In 1954, Shapley retired as director of the Observatory. If Payne-Gaposchkin had been a man, she would probably have been named his successor. As it was, the new director, Donald Menzel, became a friend. Menzel convinced the new president of Harvard to make Cecilia Payne-Gaposchkin a Harvard professor and chair of the Department of Astronomy, the first woman full professor or department chair at Harvard. To celebrate the occasion, Payne-Gaposchkin sent hand-written notes to all the young women in astronomy, inviting them to a reception in the library. There, tall as ever and by this time rather plump, she delighted them by saying, "I find myself cast in the unlikely role of a thin wedge." Perhaps the wedge proved thinner than she would have liked, since even today, only four of twenty-two faculty in the Harvard Department of Astronomy are women.

During the 1950s, Payne–Gaposhckin continued her study of variable stars, extending her work with over two million observations of stars in the Magellanic Clouds, two dwarf galaxies in the southern hemisphere. From her measurements she made inferences about the evolution and life cycle of stars. Based on this work, she wrote a popular book called *Stars in the Making,* as well as three academic books, *Variable Stars and Galactic Structures, Introduction to Astronomy, and The Galactic Novae.* She continued to build the field of astrophysics, supervising several graduate students who went on to make important contributions to the study of star formation, globular clus-ters, and SETI, the Search for Extraterrestrial Intelligence.

Payne-Gaposchkin officially retired from Harvard in 1966. As a professor *emerita*, she contin-ued to work at the Smithsonian Astronomical Observatory, which shared the grounds of the Harvard Observatory. Music and theater were still important to her. In the 1970s, she wrote an autobiography called *The Dyer's Hand,* which she published pri-vately. In 1979, she and Sergei took a last trip around the world, visiting Tahiti, Australia, India, and Turkey. By the last stages of

CECILIA

the trip, Payne-Gaposchkin was obviously ill. A chain smoker all her adult life, she had developed lung cancer. Her children played recordings of Mozart and Handel for her during her last days. After her death, they followed her wishes by donating her body to science.

Astronomer and historian of science Owen Gingerich has called Cecilia Payne-Gaposchkin "probably the most eminent woman astronomer of all time." Arriving from England with an excellent education and a two-year fellowship, she was able to establish herself as an independent researcher at a Harvard that until that time had regarded women only as "computers," skilled enough to carry out exacting routine tasks but not creative enough to develop their own theories and questions. Payne-Gaposchkin's career overturned that sex-based hierarchy. Her knowledge of quantum and atomic physics allowed her to analyze the chemical composition of the stars and to relate their spectra to physical conditions of temperature and pressure. By demonstrating that stars are made mostly of hydrogen and helium, she laid the groundwork for understanding nuclear fusion as the source of stellar radiation. That understanding in turn eventually led to the revelation that we are all made of the stuff of stars and supernovae.

ASTRONOMY

Timeline | 1903-1972

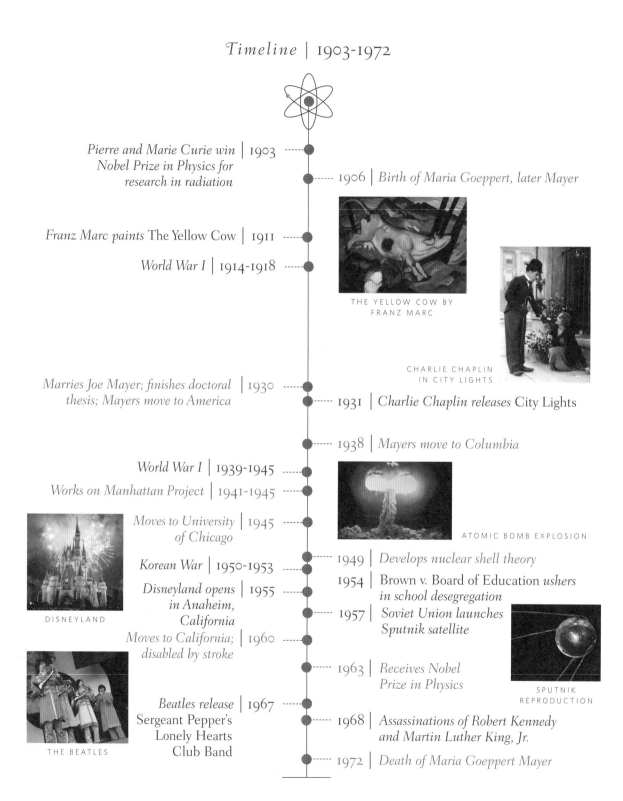

Pierre and Marie Curie win | 1903
Nobel Prize in Physics for
research in radiation

1906 | Birth of Maria Goeppert, later Mayer

Franz Marc paints The Yellow Cow | 1911

World War I | 1914-1918

THE YELLOW COW BY
FRANZ MARC

CHARLIE CHAPLIN
IN CITY LIGHTS

Marries Joe Mayer; finishes doctoral | 1930
thesis; Mayers move to America

1931 | Charlie Chaplin releases City Lights

1938 | Mayers move to Columbia

World War I | 1939-1945

Works on Manhattan Project | 1941-1945

Moves to University | 1945
of Chicago

ATOMIC BOMB EXPLOSION

1949 | Develops nuclear shell theory

Korean War | 1950-1953

1954 | Brown v. Board of Education ushers
in school desegregation

Disneyland opens | 1955
in Anaheim,
California

1957 | Soviet Union launches
Sputnik satellite

DISNEYLAND

Moves to California; | 1960
disabled by stroke

1963 | Receives Nobel
Prize in Physics

SPUTNIK
REPRODUCTION

Beatles release | 1967
Sergeant Pepper's
Lonely Hearts
Club Band

1968 | Assassinations of Robert Kennedy
and Martin Luther King, Jr.

THE BEATLES

1972 | Death of Maria Goeppert Mayer

13 | *Nuclear Shell Model*

Maria Goeppert Mayer

1906-1972 | *Germany and United States*

In the fall of 1929, Maria Goeppert traveled to the Netherlands with her fiancé Joe Mayer to visit a physicist, Paul Ehrenfest. Lively, sociable, and given to procrastination, Maria chatted happily to Ehrenfest about the doctoral thesis she meant to start sometime soon. All at once, Ehrenfest interrupted her. "You've talked enough. Now write," he told her, and he shut her into the guest room, instructing her not to come out without an outline.

The room was curiously decorated. Ehrenfest and his wife had run out of money before they finished, so instead of wallpaper Ehrenfest had simply hung up a pocket watch and asked his friends to sign the wall. With the autographs of famous scientists watching over her, Maria solved a key problem "within an hour" and left the room with her doctoral thesis in her head, ready to go. Before leaving the room, she signed the wall.

Maria Gertrud Käte Goeppert was born on June 28, 1906 in the Prussian city of Kattowitz, then part of Germany but now found in Poland. She was the

FRIEDRICH MAYER, MARIAS'S FATHER

only child of Friedrich Goeppert, a sixth-generation university professor, and his wife Maria Wolff Goeppert. When the young Maria was four years old, her father became professor of pediatrics in the university town of Göttingen on the Leine River in central Germany. Her father's position and her mother's gift for lavish entertaining gave Maria the status almost of a princess. Her father doted on her, taking her on science walks to hunt for fossils or study the moon. When she was seven, he made her dark glasses so she could watch a solar eclipse. Maria's father told her that she must have a profession and never become just "a housewife interested only in her children."

When Maria was eight, World War I began, and the family fortunes dipped. By the end of the war they were dining on turnip soup to save food for the children in Professor Mayer's hospital and day care center. At the end of the war, Maria's homeland of Upper Silesia was transferred to Poland, a move to which she never reconciled herself.

To prepare for university, Maria attended a small, private school called the *Frauenstudium* that had been established by suffragettes. When it had to close because of rampant inflation after the war, she resolved to take the university entrance examination a year early. She and four other girls passed the exam and entered the university, where Maria studied mathematics under such famous mathematicians as David Hilbert and Emmy Noether. Most women studying mathematics in Germany at the time were planning to fill a shortage of teachers in girls' schools, but Maria had something more in mind. At one of Hilbert's Sunday lectures, given in his back garden, she first heard about the new ideas of quantum physics. She found herself captivated by the "young and exciting" field, and soon decided to pursue a doctorate in physics.

Maria had a gift for making friends, and two of Göttingen's pioneers of quantum mechanics, Max Born and James Franck, came to look on her as a member of their families. Her combination of intelligence and playfulness captivated them. Born wrote of her, "Maria was a lovely and lively young girl and, when she appeared in my class, I was rather astonished. She went through all my courses with great industry and conscientiousness, yet remained at the same time a gay and witty member of 'Göttingen society,' fond of parties, of laughing, dancing, joking."

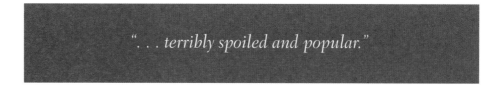

Maria's closest friends were fellow students, among them several future stars in nuclear physics. Many of them fell in love with her. She was slim, small, pretty, and flirtatious. Besides, as she later said, "Professors' daughters were tops in society and were terribly spoiled and popular." When her mother began taking in student boarders in 1927, one of the boarders was the Californian Joseph Mayer, who had come to study with Franck and Born. Mayer was impressed by Maria's English, which she had polished during a term at Cambridge. Her enthusiasm for skiing, swimming, tennis, and dancing captivated him. Joe had advantages of his own, among them a good supply of gin and a convertible. Most of all, like Maria's father, he wanted her to become a professor. Throughout their life together he encouraged and even prodded her to keep pursuing physics.

Joe and Maria married in January 1930. Energized by her visit to the Netherlands, Maria Mayer completed her doctoral thesis in March. The thesis explored double photon processes, calculating the probability that an electron orbiting a nucleus would fall two levels in energy, thus emitting two photons at once. Physicist Eugene Wigner later called the thesis a "masterpiece of clarity and concreteness." Although at the time Mayer's thesis could not be tested, work with lasers in the 1960s confirmed her theoretical findings.

A month later, the Mayers were on their way to America. Johns Hopkins University had offered Joe an assistant professorship in Baltimore. Unfortunately, nepotism rules and the Depression prevented the university from also offering Maria a paid position. Instead, she was given such titles as "fellow by courtesy" or "voluntary associate" and offered a tiny attic office. Still, she worked, with Joe's encouragement and for the simple love of physics. Together the couple entertained, sailed, hiked and even crushed grapes for wine in an old washing machine. They had two children, Marianne, born in 1933, and Peter, born in 1938.

Physics at Hopkins at the time was more geared to experiment than theory and more geared to classical physics than the new quantum mechanics. Maria turned toward chemistry, becoming interested in how quantum mechanics could help explain chemical bonds and structures. Along with

JOE AND MARIA MAYER

Joe and physicist Karl Herzfeld, she delved into the new field of physical chemistry. Maria's mathematical background in group theory and matrices gave her powerful tools of analysis. In order to keep her physics sharp, she spent the first few summers back in Göttingen working with her thesis advisor, Max Born. Extending the work of her thesis, she wrote a paper on double beta decay, describing the conditions under which a radioactive atom would emit two electrons at once.

At Hopkins, Maria's work paid off. With a graduate student named Alfred Sklar, she wrote an important paper on the structure of organic compounds. Eventually her colleagues at Hopkins managed to pay her a few hundred dollars a year to help with their German correspondence. She was also allowed to lecture, which she did nervously, speaking fast, holding a piece of chalk in one hand and her ever-present cigarette in the other. The young woman who had been so confident and outgoing in Germany had become very shy in America. Her name was not listed in the course catalog; her lectures appeared under only the initial "G." Still, she took on a graduate student, Robert Sachs, and when she helped introduce him to Edward Teller so he could learn nuclear physics, she began to learn it too. Together Mayer and Sachs wrote a paper on mesons, subatomic particles thought to be involved in holding the nucleus together.

Aware that not every man in the physics department welcomed her, Mayer tried to keep a low profile. When Karl Herzfeld asked to have her name included on the physics department's stationery, the department chair was so outraged he removed all names but his own. Mayer professed not to mind. One advantage to her unofficial status was that she felt free to take time off whenever she wished. She took a long leave when her daughter Marianne was born. But in 1938, when she stopped work a second time during her pregnancy with her son Peter, she grew weary of domestic-

MAYER WITH DAUGHTER MARIANNE

ity. Planning meals and feigning interest in neighborhood small talk bored her to tears. To her relief, Joe set her to work on a textbook they would write together, *Statistical Mechanics*. Published in 1940, the book was used by students for the next forty years.

In 1938, in a frenzy of belt-tightening, Hopkins fired a number of first-class scholars, among them Joe Mayer. Maria felt certain that her annoying presence in the physics department hadn't helped. She resolved to be even more careful in the future, letting others publish before her and avoiding any chance, as her daughter later said, that she could "be accused of being a conniving, abrasive woman."

Almost immediately, Joe was offered a position at Columbia University at twice his former salary. Maria was offered office space and the chance to be an unpaid lecturer in physics. She took it. Her neighbors in the department and in the New Jersey suburb where they lived included Edward Teller, later father of the hydrogen bomb; Harold Urey, who discovered deuterium and theorized about how life could arise from inorganic matter; and Enrico Fermi, who had fled with his Jewish wife from Fascist Italy. The Mayers threw their house open to visiting students and lecturers, and Maria chain-smoked as she talked physics with a wide range of scientists. Still, although Maria was welcome to attend departmental seminars, she was excluded from the all-male dinners that followed. She didn't mind; she went off to the opera with Edward Teller instead.

In late 1941, Maria Mayer finally got a paying job, teaching math and physics courses to women at Sarah Lawrence College. After Pearl Harbor, she also took over Fermi's lecture courses at Columbia as he was called away to work on defense projects. Then Urey, a manager for the Manhattan Project, asked her to help. Columbia was responsible for finding a way to separate fissionable uranium-235 from the more abundant uranium-238. Urey assigned Mayer to a side project investigating whether one could separate isotopes by photochemical reactions. Although the approach never worked, the experience put Maria on an equal footing with male scientists; indeed, she ended up leading a team of fifteen men, mostly chemists. Even so, she managed to get home in time to read her children bedtime stories every night, and her weekends were free. Despite her commitment to America developing a nuclear weapon before Germany did, Mayer later expressed relief that

YELLOWCAKE URANIUM

Naturally occurring uranium contains 99.28 percent uranium-238 and only about 0.71 percent of the more radioactive, less stable uranium-235. Uranium must be "enriched" to two to twenty percent U-235 by weight to be useful for nuclear reactors. Nuclear weapons require much higher purification, with forty to eighty percent U-235 by weight.

Different isotopes of the same atom react chemically in the same way, since they differ only in their number of neutrons, and neutrons are not involved in chemical reactions. Therefore, it is extremely difficult to separate the different isotopes of uranium. However, different isotopes do differ slightly in weight and density. This difference means that nuclear engineers can use ultrafast centrifuges to spin a gaseous compound of uranium and fluoride. The heavier, denser molecules containing mostly U-238 move to the outer rim of a spinning cylinder, while the lighter molecules, richer in U-235, stay toward the center of the cylinder.

EDWARD TELLER, FATHER OF THE HYDROGEN BOMB

The Argonne National Laboratory
began as Enrico Fermi's "Metallurgical Laboratory," part of the Manhattan Project to build a nuclear bomb. The laboratory built the first nuclear reactor under the stands of a sports stadium at the University of Chicago. After the war, the Metallurgical Laboratory was renamed the Argonne National Library and moved to a new location outside of Chicago.

Argonne focused at first on designing nuclear reactors to generate energy. It also explored other areas of basic physics and chemistry. Argonne researchers helped to develop ultrasound imaging and design the first nuclear-powered submarine. Research continues today in areas as diverse as supercomputers, high-energy light sources, nanoscience, alternative fuels, and understanding the local effects of climate change.

ARGONNE NATIONAL LABORATORY

MARIA MAYER

her approach had failed, since it spared her the guilt other contributors suffered after the Americans bombed Hiroshima and Nagasaki.

After the war, Joe was elected to the National Academy of Sciences and recruited to the University of Chicago, where the whole fraternity of nuclear physicists seemed to be congregating. Once more Maria picked up and moved; once more, she was offered nothing but an unpaid position. This time, the position came with faculty status. Moreover, her former PhD student Robert Sachs had been appointed head of the physics division at the new Argonne National Laboratory, which the Department of Energy had tasked with the challenge of developing peaceful nuclear power. Sachs recruited Mayer, who accepted the half-time job and set out to learn a new field. At the same time, she taught a seminar in physics theory.

A part of the physics community at last, Maria thrived. She and Joe threw grand parties reminiscent of her mother's, with three floors of their house thrown open to a hundred guests. Drink flowed freely, and Maria smoked and drank at the center of a group of scientists. At other times she attended parties that were otherwise all male.

Meanwhile, Mayer was working on a new problem that fascinated her. Why were some isotopes stable and abundant while others were unstable and rare? Clearly, the unstable ones broke down into the stable ones, but why? She collated the wealth of data gathered on isotopes during the war and noticed an odd fact. Certain numbers of protons or neutrons in the nucleus appeared to confer stability. Although others had noticed a few of these "magic numbers" of stability before, Mayer compiled a much more complete list. Atoms with 2, 8, 20, 28, 50, 82, or 126 protons or neutrons in their nucleus were endpoints. They didn't decay. The more she investigated these isotopes, along with their binding energies and spins, the more convinced she became that they supported a model of the nucleus that included stable "shells," just like the electron shells that, when filled, provided stability to atoms and compounds. In 1948, Mayer published a paper with her evidence. Only one thing was missing—a theory to explain her model.

ENRICO FERMI

One day Mayer and Fermi were discussing the problem in her office when Fermi had to go take a long-distance call. On his way out, he asked over his shoulder, "Incidentally, is there any evidence of spin-orbit coupling?" As Maria later recalled, as soon as Fermi asked the question the problem began to solve itself. She felt almost dizzy with her sudden understanding as the pieces arranged themselves in her mind. As Joe Mayer later told the story,

> *"Tomorrow, when you are less excited,*
> *you can explain it to me."*
> –Enrico Fermi

> *[Fermi] returned less than ten minutes later and Maria started to "snow" him with the detailed explanation. You may remember that Maria, when excited, had a rapid-fire oral delivery, whereas Enrico always wanted a slow detailed and methodical explanation. Enrico smiled and left: "Tomorrow, when you are less excited, you can explain it to me."*

Indeed, within a week Fermi was teaching Mayer's new theory to his seminar class.

Mayer's nuclear shell model refers by analogy to electron shells. Just as atoms with full electron shells are less likely to form compounds, nuclei with either full neutron shells or full proton shells—or better yet, both—are extremely stable. Mayer attempted to create a conceptual image of a filled nuclear shell by describing pairs of dancers, representing protons and neutrons, twirling clockwise or counterclockwise as they circle a ballroom, also in two directions. The waltz of the nucleons is a fanciful rendering of fantastically complex equations involving angular momentum, the strong nuclear force, and more. What is impressive is how well the nuclear shell model predicts other properties of the atomic nucleus related to nuclear spin, parity, and magnetism.

Delighted as she was by her discovery, Mayer dragged her feet about publishing it. At first she wanted Fermi to be co-author because his question had enlightened her, but he refused to absorb

MARIA MAYER

part of her glory. Then she heard of another group that planned to present their own attempt at an explanation, and ever gallant, she asked the editor of *Physical Review* to hold back her own letter until it could appear simultaneously with theirs. As a result, unfortunately, her paper appeared one issue later than that of a German group, led by Hans Jensen, whose interpretation was almost identical to hers.

At first dismayed, Mayer soon decided that two papers were better than one, and that together she and Jensen could convince the nuclear physics community of a theory so different from past accepted models. Indeed, she and Jensen soon met, and instead of becoming rivals, they became fast friends. They deferred to each other over the theory, each referring to it as *"your* theory." Maria called Jensen "a dear, gentle man," while he considered her "unbelievably modest." Together they produced a book about the shell model, with Maria writing eighty percent of it. At Jensen's insistence, Mayer's name appeared first on the title page.

In 1956, Maria Mayer was finally elected to the National Academy of Sciences, ten years after her husband. She was the fifth woman so honored. By then Fermi had died, and the Chicago physics group was scattering. Urey moved to the new University of California San Diego and invited the Mayers to follow. This time the university offered Maria a full professorship with pay. All at once, the University of Chicago found some money and matched the offer. It was too late. The Mayers moved to California in 1960.

Then, while unpacking her books in their new home, Maria Mayer suffered a stroke. She lost the use of her left arm, and her speech became blurred. Her health never recovered. Still, she continued to teach as long as she could and continued to work elucidating the shell model. In 1963, she was awarded the Nobel Prize in Physics along with Jensen and her old Göttingen friend Eugene Wigner. The local paper hardly knew what to do with the news, announcing "S. D. Mother Wins Nobel Prize."

> *"If you love science, all you really want is to keep working."*

In Stockholm, an aide stood nearby to carry Mayer's medal and diploma. Then King Gustav VI Adolf took her arm, and people sank to their knees as he escorted her though the reception hall into dinner. It was a fairy-tale ending to a Cinderella career. Maria Mayer treasured the moment, but as she said afterward, "If you love science, all you really want is to keep on working. The Nobel Prize thrills you, but it changes nothing." Unfortunately, her declining health made work increasingly difficult, and she died on February 20, 1972.

Brilliant and lively, sociable and astute, Maria Mayer suffered setbacks throughout her career because of her gender. Yet in many ways she was lucky. In Germany she would never have had the opportunities she found in America. She was blessed with a husband who cared about her career almost more than she did. His success allowed her to continue doing physics even when it paid nothing or next to nothing. And despite the institutions and bureaucrats that barred her way, she always had a circle of physicists who respected and even loved her as one of their own.

Timeline | 1906-2012

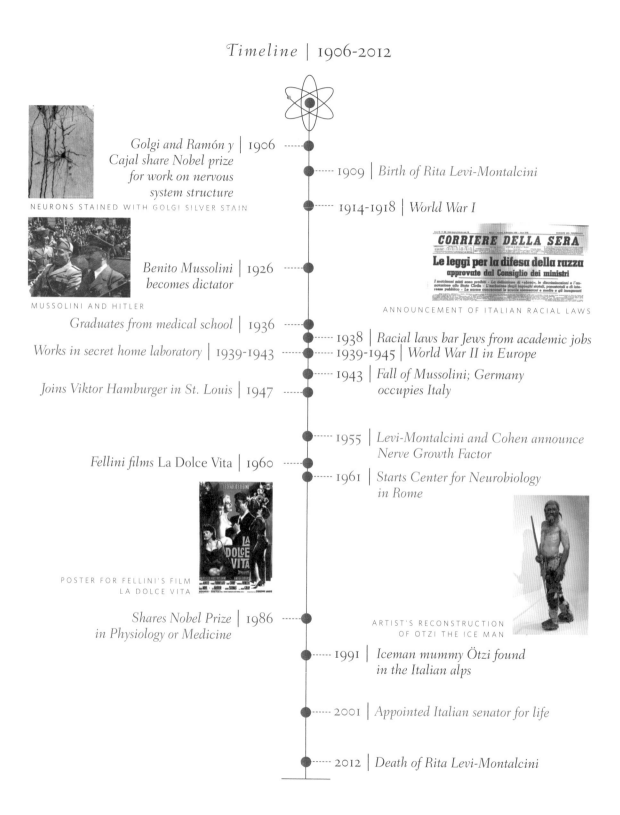

Golgi and Ramón y | 1906
Cajal share Nobel prize
for work on nervous
system structure

NEURONS STAINED WITH GOLGI SILVER STAIN

1909 | Birth of Rita Levi-Montalcini

1914-1918 | World War I

CORRIERE DELLA SERA
Le leggi per la difesa della razza
approvate dal Consiglio dei ministri

Benito Mussolini | 1926
becomes dictator

MUSSOLINI AND HITLER

ANNOUNCEMENT OF ITALIAN RACIAL LAWS

Graduates from medical school | 1936

1938 | Racial laws bar Jews from academic jobs

Works in secret home laboratory | 1939-1943

1939-1945 | World War II in Europe

1943 | Fall of Mussolini; Germany
occupies Italy

Joins Viktor Hamburger in St. Louis | 1947

1955 | Levi-Montalcini and Cohen announce
Nerve Growth Factor

Fellini films La Dolce Vita | 1960

1961 | Starts Center for Neurobiology
in Rome

POSTER FOR FELLINI'S FILM
LA DOLCE VITA

Shares Nobel Prize | 1986
in Physiology or Medicine

ARTIST'S RECONSTRUCTION
OF OTZI THE ICE MAN

1991 | Iceman mummy Ötzi found
in the Italian alps

2001 | Appointed Italian senator for life

2012 | Death of Rita Levi-Montalcini

14 | *Nerve Growth Factor*

Rita Levi-Montalcini

1909-2012 | *Italy and United States*

Rita Levi-Montalcini, a visiting scientist at Washington University of St. Louis, felt discouraged. It was 1947, and she was thirty-eight years old. An Italian Jew, she had lost ten years of her career to Fascism and war. Worse yet, now that she had returned to research, she doubted her choice of field. Although she had done important work in embryology during the most difficult of circumstances during the war, now she felt that her studies of nervous system development in the embryo had stalled. She envied her medical school friends who had concentrated in microbiology, because they could do so many more experiments than she could manage with her chick embryos. She even mused about whether she should change fields. Her friends advised her that it was probably too late.

Then, in the course of one glorious afternoon, Levi-Montalcini's optimism returned. Peering through the microscope at slides taken from the spinal cords of

RITA LEVI-MONTALCINI LECTURING IN 2008

chick embryos in the first week of life, she suddenly perceived a pattern that gave new meaning to her observations of the past several years. In successive slides prepared from embryos only a few hours apart, she saw two columns of nerve cells progressing, like an army marching from one part of the spinal cord to another. Then some of the trailing cells died, their nuclear membranes dissolving and their cell bodies shrinking away. Finally, macrophages, the blood's janitorial cells, arrived to devour the debris. The image that formed in Levi-Montalcini's imagination was one of "corpses being removed from the battlefield by special crews trained and equipped for the purpose." All at once, the development of the nervous system appeared to Levi-Montalcini as a dynamic, orchestrated, and meaningful process. For the first time, she had not just observed neurons growing in place, migrating to a new spot, or even dying in place. Instead, she had seen the body actively pruning away excess neurons as part of normal development. Excited, she summoned her supervisor and host, Viktor Hamburger, to see. Once she had shared her discovery, she put a Bach cantata on the record player and, full of joy, rededicated herself to studying the nervous system.

Rita Levi-Montalcini was born in 1909 to a wealthy and educated Jewish family in Turin, a city in the industrial north of Italy. She and her fraternal twin sister Paola had an older brother who became an architect and an older sister with a talent for writing. Their father Adamo Levi was an engineer and factory owner who manufactured ice, distilled liquor, and ruled the family down to the details of which hats the girls should wear. He raised his children as freethinkers, telling them they could decide as adults whether they wanted to be Jewish or Catholic. To please his wife, he consented to participating in the annual Passover meal at the homes of her relatives, but he always disrupted the Seder during the description of the plagues God visited on Egypt, crying, "What hatred!" He was given to towering rages that quickly passed. Rita feared him, but she admired his resoluteness and energy. Although she felt much closer to her meek mother, who had set aside her identity as an artist to raise a family, Rita decided early that the role of wife and mother was not for her.

For four years, Rita and Paola attended an elementary school where classes were segregated by gender. When the twins were in first grade, Italy entered World War I on the side of England and France, and Rita dreamed of becoming a Red Cross nurse. Not many other options appeared open to her. Her male cousins taunted her, telling her that all the great intellects of history had been men.

After elementary school, the Levi-Montalcini boys were sent to schools that could prepare them for university, while the girls were sent to finishing schools meant to prepare them for family life. Paola, always quiet, simply concentrated on her painting. Rita, who felt no particular aptitude for any subject, finished school at seventeen and languished at home, feeling trapped and unhappy. Then, as she describes in her autobiography, their beloved nanny Giovanna fell ill and died a painful death of stomach cancer. Coming away from the deathbed, Rita resolved to study medicine.

Adamo Levi disapproved. Medicine, he said, was a hard course and unsuitable for a woman. But Rita, now twenty years old and just as stubborn as her father, prevailed. She persuaded her cousin Eugenia to join her, and they committed themselves to preparing for the university entrance exams in just eight months. They hired one tutor for Greek and Latin and another for science and mathematics. History and literature they studied on their own. The two young women spent the summer in a mountain village, where Rita roused her cousin at four every morning to study. When

LEVI-MONTALCINI FAMILY. THE TWINS PAOLA AND RITA ARE IN FRONT.

autumn came, the two cousins passed the examination and entered a medical school class of three hundred men and seven women.

Meanwhile, the family fortunes were in decline. Adamo's ice factory and liquor distillery in Bari had failed, despite loans from relatives; he worked fiendishly to rebuild his business in Turin. He refused to let increasing chest pains or even warning signs of stroke stop him, until in 1932 he became disabled by heart failure. As he was dying, he sat up in a chair with his family around him, reciting Dante's *Divine Comedy*. When he died, Rita was devastated.

At medical school, where the young men ogled the women and rated their attractiveness, Rita dressed conservatively and tried to ignore them. One student later told her that in medical school she was like "a kind of squid ready to squirt ink at anybody who came near you." She allowed one young man to take her on long walks as long as he promised to avoid romance and converse only about art and culture. Meanwhile, she chose for her mentor a man who in many ways resembled her father. Giuseppe Levi was tall, red-haired, and sloppy in his dress. He had bushy eyebrows and a fearsome temper, and he was a courageous and outspoken anti-Fascist. Though he taught the freshman anatomy course, his real field was the histology, or microscopic anatomy, of the nervous system. Many students sought to become his research assistants.

Professor Levi, whom Rita always called the Master, assigned Eugenia and Rita the tedious task of counting cells in mouse sensory ganglia. Ganglia are clusters of nerve cells found outside the

COLLAGEN MOLECULES
FORM A TRIPLE HELIX

brain or spinal cord, and Levi wanted to know if the numbers of neurons they included was constant in different mice. When they had finished the counting task—several other students told Rita they simply gave up and fudged the counts—the Master came up with another project for them. Rita's was to study how the convolutions of the brain form in the human fetus. It was a hopeless task: there were no human fetuses to study. Levi raged at Rita's failure, calling her work "real trash" and pronouncing that she was not cut out for research. But later, after she fell ill and required an operation, he relented and gave her a new project. Using tissue culture, growing sheets of cells in glass dishes, she studied the formation of collagen fibers. In her research and subsequent doctoral thesis, Rita was able to show that these strong protein fibers, which provide structural support for most of the body, are created by a number of different kinds of tissue, including muscle and skin.

In 1936, Rita Levi-Montalcini graduated from medical school and began an internship in neurology and psychiatry. She continued her research, becoming expert in the technique of silver staining, which made individual neurons stand out clearly in dark brown against a light tan background. As much as she could, she ignored the political situation. Benito Mussolini had come to power fourteen years earlier, and in 1925 he had established a dictatorship, abolishing the free press and outlawing opposition parties. Many of his political opponents were arrested or fled into exile. Rita's Master Giuseppe Levi, who loudly mocked Fascist policies on the trams and in other public places, was briefly arrested after his son was found carrying anti-Fascist leaflets into the country from Switzerland.

In 1936, Italian newspaper articles began a concerted attack on the country's Jews, and in 1938 the "racial laws" were passed, forbidding marriage between Jews and Aryans and barring Jews from any academic or government posts. Levi-Montalcini officially lost her job at Turin's Clinic for Nervous and Mental Diseases. For a while she kept going to work anyway—with her colleagues concealing her presence—but in March 1939 she moved to Brussels to continue her research there. Then, in September, Germany invaded Poland and threatened Belgium. Believing that Italy would remain at peace, Rita Levi-Montalcini returned home.

For a while, Levi-Montalcini tried practicing medicine illegally among some of her former patients, but she constantly needed to call on Aryan friends to write prescriptions. The situation was untenable; she was putting her friends at risk. Thwarted in her attempts to be useful, Levi-Montalcini found herself sitting at home with nothing to do. She was beginning to sink into self-pity when a friend from medical school came and asked her what

"One doesn't lose heart in the face of the first difficulties . . ."
−A classmate of Rita Levi-Montalcini

she was studying. He scolded her for her inactivity, saying, "One doesn't lose heart in the face of the first difficulties. Set up a small laboratory and take up your interrupted research. Remember Ramón y Cajal who in a poorly equipped institute, in the sleepy city [of] Valencia . . . did the fundamental work that established the basis of all we know about the nervous system of vertebrates."

Encouraged by this advice, Levi-Montalcini set to work. Her brother Gino built her an incubator, a glass box with two circular openings in front so she could reach inside. The incubator had a small thermostat and was warmed to body temperature; another box was kept hotter for fixing tissue in paraffin or hot wax. Rita acquired two microscopes, forceps, and tiny scissors. She ground sewing needles into tiny surgical tools. Once she set up her laboratory in a corner of her bedroom, Rita bought fertilized eggs and began to stain and study the nervous systems of chick embryos. Meanwhile, threats and denouncements of Jews continued. Levi-Montalcini's Master Giuseppe Levi, also returned from Belgium, arrived daily to assist her in her tiny laboratory.

One day, Levi-Montalcini read a scientific paper on a train. The passenger cars were used for troop transport, so ordinary people rode on open-sided livestock cars. Rita read as she sat with her legs hanging over the side, smelling the fresh-cut hay of the countryside. The paper, by Viktor Hamburger, related what happened when he surgically removed a limb bud, the first little bulging growth of what was programmed to become a leg or wing, in a chick embryo. In Hamburger's samples, the sensory ganglion destined to send nerve fibers to that excised limb appeared much smaller than usual. Hamburger thought the limb was producing some substance that induced the ganglion to grow. Without the substance, the ganglion remained underdeveloped. Levi-Montalcini rushed to her bedroom laboratory to reproduce the experiments.

By the second half of 1942, Turin was a target of Allied bombing, and Levi-Montalcini frequently had to carry her slides and microscope to the cellar to wait out a bombing raid. Eventually the family moved to a small village in the hills, where Rita re-established her lab setup in a corner of the shared living and dining room. She bought eggs from neighboring farmers, asking for fertile ones because they would be "healthier" for the child she pretended to have. When she finished studying the eggs she scrambled them into omelets for the family supper.

CHICK EMBRYO, ONE WEEK OLD. WIKIMEDIA COMMONS

MUSSOLINI AND HITLER

Benito Mussolini came to power in Italy in 1922, but he did not act against the Jews until 1938. The small Jewish minority in Italy was well integrated into Italian life, and anti-Semitism in Italy was uncommon. However, Mussolini's desire to cement the alliance between Italy and Germany led him to embrace Hitler's racial theories.

After a press campaign and publication of a pseudo-scientific Manifesto of Race, Italy passed its **Racial Laws in November 1938**. *The laws barred Jews from public office or higher education, banned their books, restricted their civil rights, and banned intermarriage between "Aryans" and Jews. Later laws restricted Jews from travel and stripped them of their assets.*

Working in her makeshift laboratory, Levi-Montalcini discovered that, contrary to Hamburger's conjecture, the ganglia meant to innervate excised limb buds did grow initially, but then shrank away again. In 1943, she wrote a paper that carefully detailed the normal growth of an embryo, with neural cells growing and moving toward each limb. Because she was a Jew, this paper could not be published in Italy, but it did appear in the Belgian literature. In 1944, she published a second paper, showing that when she removed an embryonic limb, the nerve cells leading to it degenerated. This time, no longer able to publish even in Belgium, Levi-Montalcini published her research through the independent Vatican state. As her classmate had counseled her to do, even during wartime she persisted in doing fundamental research and finding a way to make it public.

On July 25, 1943, Mussolini resigned. There was jubilation in the streets until, in reaction, Germany invaded Italy, meaning all Jews were now in mortal danger. Levi-Montalcini's sister and husband fled across the border to Switzerland, but the rest of the family were too late. With forged documents, they fled south, ending up in Florence. There they lodged with a family who pretended to believe they were not Jews, even when Professor Giuseppe Levi showed up once more and asked to be announced as "Professor Levi—I mean Lovitano!" As the Allies advanced from the south, Italian partisans fought the Germans, the Germans blew up the bridges of Florence, and the English army finally reached Florence on September 2, 1944.

During the final days of the war, Levi-Montalcini volunteered to work with the Allies as a doctor. She saw patients in a clinic with straw scattered over a dirt floor. Her patients were peasant families transported back from the front, suffering from cold, malnutrition and dehydration. An outbreak of typhoid fever killed hundreds, and there was little the medical staff could do but isolate the dying so they would not infect others. To see such suffering without being able to help devastated Levi-Montalicini. By the end of her term, she knew she did not have the detachment needed to practice medicine.

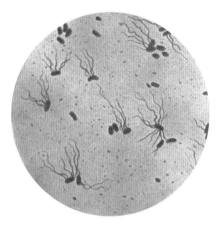

SALMONELLA TYPHI, THE BACILLUS
THAT CAUSES TYPHOID FEVER

When the war ended, Levi-Montalcini returned to Turin. Some friends and relatives had perished and others had emigrated. The country was poor; research opportunities were bleak. Levi-Montalcini enrolled in a course of biology to strengthen her basic knowledge. Then, to her surprise, she received a letter from Viktor Hamburger, who had read her papers on ganglions and limb buds. He invited her to spend a semester as a visiting scientist in St. Louis. Levi-Montalcini jumped at the chance. After completing her biology studies in 1947, she took a ship to New York and a train to St. Louis.

Levi-Montalcini immediately felt comfortable with Victor Hamburger, a German Jew who had fled Germany for the United States. Though he towered over the diminutive Levi-Montalcini, he had none of the domineering attitude of her previous mentors. He helped her find lodging with a landlady who confided to her refined new Italian tenant how much she hated Jews. Levi-Montalcini gloried in Washington University's huge library, where one could stay until all hours. When not working, she took boat rides on the Mississippi, went on picnics, or visited Bloomington to talk with her friends from student days, Renato Dulbecco and Salvador Luria, both future Nobel Prize winners. Best of all, the day she saw the pattern of marching armies through her microscope, she regained her faith in experimental neuroembryology. She decided to stay in St. Louis.

In 1950, Hamburger showed Levi-Montalcini a letter from a former student. The student described experiments he had abandoned a couple of years earlier but still wondered about. He had been implanting tumors into chick embryos when he noticed a sudden overgrowth of nerve fibers that he couldn't explain. Her curiosity aroused, Levi-Montalcini ordered some mice with tumors and transplanted small chunks of mouse tumor into her chick embryos. The results astounded her. She found nerve fibers growing from ganglia in all directions but especially toward the tumors, even invading the embryo veins that drained the tumors. She later wrote, "These fiber bundles passed

VIKTOR HAMBURGER IN 1933

> *". . . like rivulets of water flowing steadily*
> *over a bed of stones . . ."*

between the cells something like rivulets of water flowing steadily over a bed of stones," not attaching to any of the cells. The striking fact that the fibers penetrated veins suggested to her that they were responding to some factor in the chick's circulation, something carried in the veins that drained the tumor.

Over the course of many years, Levi-Montalcini pursued this factor. Carrying two mice in her pocketbook, she traveled to Brazil, where her old schoolmate Hertha Mayer was perfecting *in vitro* ("in glass") techniques. Working with cells in culture, Levi-Montalcini eventually found that after tumor cells had been growing for a while, even fluid from the plates they grew on could stimulate nerve cells. The nerve cells sprouted a strikingly beautiful "halo" of nerve fibers, and Levi-Montalcini was elated.

No such factor as the one she was observing had been described before. Here was a factor found in a tissue extract that led to exuberant growth in a completely unrelated tissue. Levi-Montalcini knew that to convince other scientists of its existence, she needed to isolate and characterize the factor. Luckily, Hamburger had just recruited a young biochemist named Stanley Cohen to join their team. Cohen smoked a pipe, played the flute, and limped as a result of childhood polio. Together, he and Levi-Montalcini formed a powerful team. Back in St. Louis, she worked for a year extracting enough factor from her glass plates for him to analyze. Cohen found that the Nerve Growth Factor (NGF) existed in a small fraction of nucleoprotein, though at first he was unable to determine whether it was protein or nucleic acid.

Advice from Arthur Kornberg, another future Nobel Prize winner, broke the impasse. Kornberg suggested treating the extract with snake venom, which broke down nucleic acid but left protein intact. The pair tried it. To their amazement, they found that snake venom itself contained NGF and led to far greater nerve fiber growth than any of their tumor extracts. Cohen reasoned that since snake venom, which was very expensive, came from snake salivary glands, maybe the salivary glands of other animals could also be a source of their mysterious factor. He proved right: an extract of mouse salivary glands carried three thousand times more factor than the tumor extracts Levi-Montalcini had labored over for so long. Now finally they had enough active material to really characterize the growth factor, and they announced their identification of NGF in 1955.

The discovery of Nerve Growth Factor opened as many questions as it answered, and Levi-Montalcini and Cohen worked together for four more years before a shortage of funding in the biology department meant that Cohen had to move on. Before leaving, he noticed that mice treated with a certain extract opened their eyes days earlier than normal. Once he moved to Vanderbilt University, his further investigations of this finding led to the discovery of Epidermal Growth Factor. Today hundreds of growth factors are known.

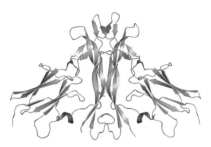

NERVE GROWTH FACTOR

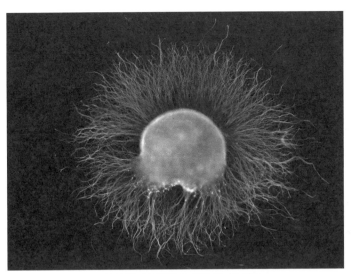

A "HALO" OF NERVE FIBERS GROWS
FROM A GANGLION

Growth factors *are molecules that carry signals between cells, and that lead target cells to grow, divide, or differentiate—that is, to become other, more mature types of cells. Most growth factors are either proteins or steroid hormones. There are now hundreds of growth hormones known, and they fall into families of molecules that are related by evolution and in the ways they act. Growth factors are important in regulating normal development, and they also play a role in healing.*

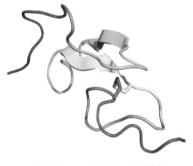

EPIDERMAL GROWTH FACTOR

Throughout her years in St. Louis, Levi-Montalcini returned to Italy for a month every summer. Eventually she decided she wanted to spend more time in her former home. While keeping her appointment at Washington University, she spent several months each year from 1961 on working to build a research institute in Rome. Her twin sister Paola came to live with her, and they renewed the closeness of their childhood years. Rita found space, attracted scientists, and administered funds. Accustomed to American informality, she was unhappily surprised to find that fellows and technicians spoke to her with the obsequious respect her own professors had demanded in the thirties. Overall, she found that Italian science still had not recovered from the war. Equipment was outdated, bureaucracy ruled, and funding was uncertain. Nevertheless, she persevered. From 1961 to 1969, she headed the Center of Neurobiology, and when the Center expanded into the Laboratory of Cell Biology, she stayed on as leader until 1978. Meanwhile, in 1971, another scientific group sequenced the amino acids in NGF. Levi-Montalcini retired in 1979, having shown that NGF had major effects on the nervous system.

Because of her discoveries, Rita Levi-Montalcini became a revered figure in Italy. She remained active in

EXTRACTING SNAKE VENOM. WIKIMEDIA COMMONS.

retirement, speaking up in support of science and the rights of women. Having progressed far from the stern shyness of her student days, she always dressed with an impeccable sense of style, and she maintained a wide circle of friends. In 1992, she established an educational foundation that eventually provided for the education of six thousand African women. Besides her scientific papers, she wrote twenty-one popular books, including an autobiography and books about biology, research ethics, and women scientists. In 1986, she and Stanley Cohen were awarded the Nobel Prize in Physiology or Medicine for their discovery of the first growth factor. Some controversy arose over the question of whether Viktor Hamburger should have shared in the prize, but Levi-Montalcini thought not. He had been a wonderful and supportive leader, she said, but he had not discovered Nerve Growth Factor.

In her retirement, Levi-Montalcini continued to contribute to science. She stressed the importance of a particular kind of blood cell, the mast cell, in contributing to the swelling and pain of inflammation. In 1993 she discovered that the compound PEA (palmitoylethanolamide), which occurs naturally in the body, helps to modulate the activity of mast cells. Her line of research led to PEA's use as an anti-inflammatory medication.

SENATOR FOR LIFE

In 2001, a liberal government appointed Rita Levi-Montalcini senator for life. She took the appointment seriously, regularly voting with the liberals. During a budget standoff in 2006, she arrived, fashionably dressed and on the arm of an usher, to cast the deciding vote approving the government budget on the condition that funding for scientific research was preserved. She was ninety-seven years old.

Rita Levi-Montalcini's last scientific paper was published in 2012. In December of that same year, at the age of 103, she died quietly at home. The mayor of Rome praised her as a representative of "civic conscience, culture, and the spirit of research of our time." Growth factors are now recognized as important messengers that allow cells to communicate with one another, thereby controlling growth and development, healing, and the immune response. It was Rita Levi-Montalcini's remarkable persistence in pursuing her research through periods of danger and discouragement that allowed her to clarify the role of these important molecules.

Timeline | 1913-2013

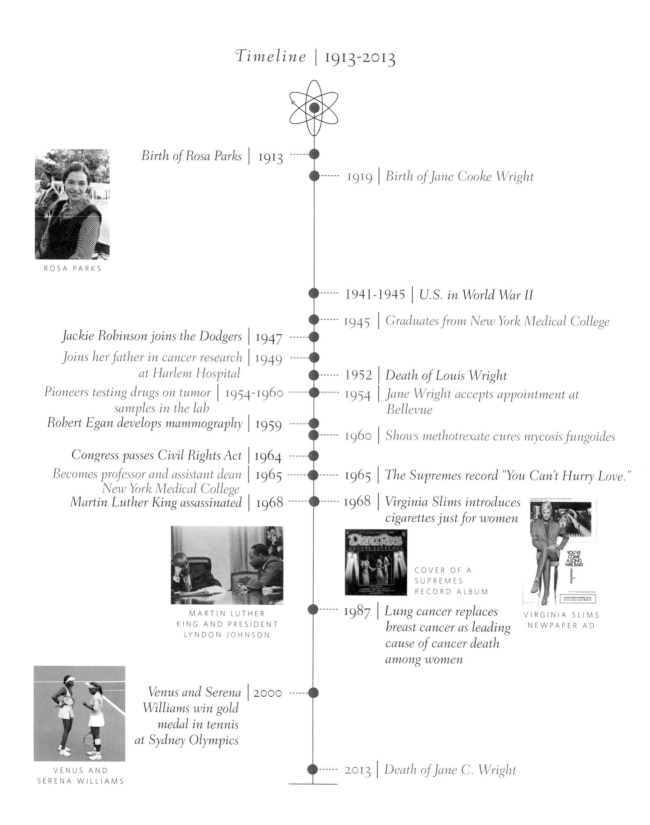

Birth of Rosa Parks | 1913

1919 | *Birth of Jane Cooke Wright*

ROSA PARKS

1941-1945 | U.S. in World War II

1945 | *Graduates from New York Medical College*

Jackie Robinson joins the Dodgers | 1947

Joins her father in cancer research | 1949
at Harlem Hospital

1952 | Death of Louis Wright

Pioneers testing drugs on tumor | 1954-1960
samples in the lab

1954 | *Jane Wright accepts appointment at Bellevue*

Robert Egan develops mammography | 1959

1960 | *Shows methotrexate cures mycosis fungoides*

Congress passes Civil Rights Act | 1964

Becomes professor and assistant dean | 1965
New York Medical College

1965 | The Supremes record "You Can't Hurry Love."

Martin Luther King assassinated | 1968

1968 | *Virginia Slims introduces cigarettes just for women*

COVER OF A
SUPREMES
RECORD ALBUM

MARTIN LUTHER
KING AND PRESIDENT
LYNDON JOHNSON

1987 | *Lung cancer replaces breast cancer as leading cause of cancer death among women*

VIRGINIA SLIMS
NEWPAPER AD

Venus and Serena | 2000
Williams win gold
medal in tennis
at Sydney Olympics

VENUS AND
SERENA WILLIAMS

2013 | *Death of Jane C. Wright*

15 | *Chemotherapy Pioneer*

Jane Cooke Wright

1919-2013 | *United States*

"Chemotherapy can be depressing," Dr. Jane Cooke Wright told a reporter in 1967. "There are many failures. But I have seen tumors vanish." She had given patients anti-cancer medicines that had cured them of Hodgkin's disease, leukemia, two kinds of skin cancer, and even breast cancer. Chemotherapy for cancer was frustratingly difficult, toxic, and unpredictable, but, said Wright, "With the right drugs cures are possible."

An African American woman, Jane Cooke came from a remarkable family of medical pioneers. In 1881 her paternal grandfather was one of the first students to graduate from Meharry Medical College, which had been established to teach medicine to former slaves. After only a few years of medical practice, he decided to become a pastor instead, and he died when Jane's father Louis was only four years old. But in 1899 Jane's grandmother Lula married again, choosing another physician. Lula's second husband, Dr. William Fletter Penn, was the first African American to receive a medical degree from Yale. Penn encouraged Jane's father, Louis Tompkins Wright, to become a doctor in his turn.

As both a surgeon and a civil rights leader, Dr. Louis Wright had a huge influence on the lives of his two daughters. Born in 1891, he graduated with highest marks from Clark University of Atlanta and sought an interview for admission to Harvard Medical School. Wright's skeptical interviewer offered to admit him if he could pass a chemistry exam; he did so. Racism dogged his course at Harvard. He had to fight to be allowed to deliver the babies of white women, and once he left school for three weeks to join protests against D.W. Griffiths' racist film, *Birth of a Nation*.

Although Louis Wright graduated fourth in his Harvard class, no Boston hospital offered him an internship. Instead, he did his surgical internship at Freedman's Hospital, a hospital for blacks

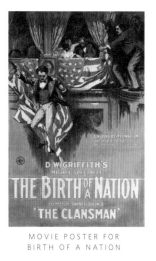

MOVIE POSTER FOR
BIRTH OF A NATION

D. W. Griffith's epic silent film **The Birth of a Nation***, released in 1915, portrayed the Ku Klux Klan as a chivalrous and heroic force restoring order to the American South following the Civil War. Three hours long, the film introduced a number of pioneering techniques, such as night shots, the use of hundreds of extras, and panoramic long shots. It featured white actors in blackface portraying black Union militiamen, thugs, and politicians. At one point, the film celebrated the lynching of a black man who had made advances to a white woman.*

The National Association for the Advancement of Colored People (NAACP), which had formed only six years earlier in 1909, organized protests and called for the film to be banned. After seeing the movie, gangs of whites attacked blacks, and in Indiana one white man murdered a black teenager. In the end, only twelve mayors banned or censored the film, which became the highest-grossing movie until Gone With the Wind *twenty-four years later. Nevertheless, protests against the film helped the NAACP recruit members and grow in influence.*

only in Washington DC. In 1917, he joined the Army Medical Corps as a lieutenant. On duty in Europe, he suffered a German gas attack, which did permanent damage to his lungs. He left the army as a captain with a Purple Heart, and in the Medical Reserves he eventually rose to the rank of lieutenant colonel.

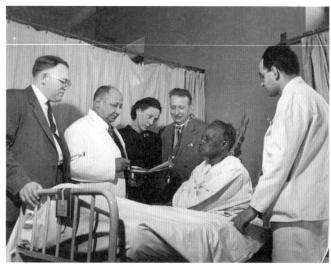

LOUIS T. WRIGHT ON ROUNDS AT HARLEM HOSPITAL

After the war, Louis Wright moved to New York, where he opened a surgical practice and married an elementary school teacher, Corinne Cook. He became the first black staff physician of any New York municipal hospital when he was appointed visiting assistant surgeon at Harlem Hospital. At that time, the hospital served primarily an affluent white community, and four white staff doctors resigned in protest at his appointment. Wright insisted that white patients call him doctor and that both doctors and patients speak with respect to black nurses, who were just beginning to be trained at Harlem Hospital.

Louis and Corinne welcomed their daughter Jane in November 1919 and Jane's sister Barbara eleven months later. At work, Louis focused on treating fractures and head injuries, for which he invented a special neck brace. In 1928 he passed the exam to become a police surgeon, and he labored to develop new approaches to knife and gunshot wounds. In 1930, Wright spoke up against plans to build special hospitals for blacks in New York City. Such hospitals, he predicted, would lead to segregated medical training and permanent second-class status for African-American medicine. "Someday," he said, "the nation will wake up to the fact that disease germs are not color conscious."

In 1937, as his daughters were entering college, Louis Wright fell ill with tuberculosis. With his gas-damaged lungs, it took him three years to overcome the disease and return to practice. By that time, he had earned the respect of his peers so completely that at his twenty-fifth medical school reunion, his Harvard classmates named him the man in the class who had made the greatest contribution to medical knowledge. Active in the early struggle for African-American rights, Wright joined the board of the National Association for the Advancement of Colored People (NAACP) and eventually became its chairman. Then, in 1948, he took on a new challenge: finding treatments for cancer. He founded a cancer research center at Harlem Hospital, where he was now director of surgery. There he tested newly developed cancer drugs on patients for whom every other treatment had failed. He also sought new treatments for a serious sexually transmitted disease called lymphgranuloma venereum, or LGV. Patients with LGV develop chronically swollen, painful, and sometimes draining lymph nodes in the groin. Wright was the first to try the antibiotic aureomycin against this disease; indeed, he was the first to test it in humans at all. It was effective.

Only four years after launching his cancer research center, Dr. Louis Tompkins Wright died of a heart attack. He was only sixty-one years old. Both daughters sought to live up to his example. Although both became doctors, they followed smoother paths than their father, facing fewer obstacles due to race or even gender than he had. Although both were brilliant and hardworking, they clearly benefited from the battles fought and won before them by their father and his peers.

As children, Jane and Barbara attended a private school, the Ethical Culture School, which later merged with its upper school, the Fieldston School. Founded in 1878, the school proudly embraced its mission: "To develop individuals who will be competent to change their environment to greater conformity with moral ideals." A strong student, Jane also loved swimming and dance. In high school she joined the Hanya Holm Dance Troupe, a professional troupe that held several performances in New York City. She also set school swimming records in the hundred-meter freestyle and breaststroke.

BARBARA AND JANE WRIGHT, AGES ONE AND TWO, FROM THE SOPHIA SMITH COLLECTION, SMITH COLLEGE.

Jane did so well in school that she won a scholarship to Smith College. The scholarship couldn't have come at a better time. The Depression had taken hold, and Louis Wright was away at a sanatorium undergoing treatment for tuberculosis. Money was short. Jane's mother Corrine made her daughters' clothes, and both girls found jobs at college. Despite having no extra money for anything except books, Jane thrived. She declared as an art major, swam on the varsity swim team, and danced in the chorus of a student production of *Electra*. But in her third year, after consult-

HARLEM HOSPITAL MURAL

ing with her father, she changed her major to pre-medicine. Although she denied ever feeling undue pressure from her father about her choice of career, Jane admitted that he had advised her to aim for a profession where she could support herself.

Because the Wrights were a prominent family in the African-American community, their successes were always well documented. When Jane Wright graduated from Smith College in 1942, her picture filled the cover page of *The Crisis: A Record of the Darker Races*, the journal of the New York branch of the NAACP.

That year, Jane Wright entered the New York Medical College on a full scholarship, the only person of color in her class. (Harvard, her father's alma mater, would not be open to women for three more years.) Because of World War II, her course of study was accelerated to three years instead of the usual four. Once more Wright thrived, becoming class treasurer and then class president, joining the honor society, serving as literary editor of the yearbook, and graduating number three in her class. A year later, her sister Barbara obtained a medical degree from Columbia.

The media continued to pay attention. The local paper published an article about the Wright sisters titled, "Beauty Goes Medical." The article quoted Jane as saying, "Race hasn't kept us from anything we wanted to do." In a photo spread in 1949, *Ebony* magazine named Jane C. Wright "one of the most beautiful Negro women in America." Authors of later articles about Jane in *Mademoiselle* and *Ladies Home Journal*, perhaps uncomfortable presenting a strong professional black woman, emphasized Wright's femininity, her good taste in clothes, and her love of cooking. An article in the *New York Weekend Post* said of Wright, "She has elfin good looks, a schoolgirl's giggle, and an insatiable appetite for work."

> *". . .by all odds the most promising intern*
> *I have ever worked with."*
> –Jane Cooke Wright's supervisor.

Upon graduation from New York Medical College, Jane Wright began a medical internship at New York's Bellevue Hospital. Her supervisor called her "by all odds the most promising intern I have ever worked with." After six months as an assistant resident, Wright, now married to a Harvard-educated lawyer named David Jones, took a leave to have a baby. She resumed work in 1947 as chief resident in medicine at Harlem Hospital, and her sister Barbara helped take care of her daughter.

After residency training, Wright took a position as a school physician for the New York City schools. She had just begun a private practice on the side when her father, who had launched his cancer research center only the year before, asked her to join him. It was a risky career move. As Dr. Ezra Jones of Mt. Sinai hospital later remembered, those practicing cancer chemotherapy in the 1940s "were generally deemed by their confreres to be dreamers, misguided fools, or charlatans." Still, Jane had the greatest respect for her father, so she signed up as a volunteer visiting physician at Harlem Hospital, while keeping her paying job with the school department. She went on hospital rounds with her father, and when surgery and radiation had nothing more to offer a cancer patient, they carefully chose and tested some new anti-cancer compound on that patient.

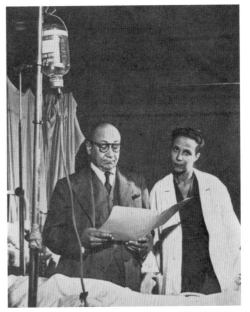

JANE WRIGHT ON ROUNDS WITH HER FATHER AT HARLEM HOSPITAL, EBONY, 1951.

One of the earliest chemotherapy treatments the Wrights tried grew out of chemical warfare. During World War II, a ship carrying the blistering chemical warfare agent nitrogen mustard sank in an Italian port, and sailors were exposed to the escaping poison gas. Many of them died; those who survived showed an alarming drop in their number of white blood cells. A group at Yale conceived the idea that a similar compound might be useful in treating leukemia, a disease in which white blood cells multiply and grow out of control. Soon Louis and Jane Wright were doing trials in Harlem on a new drug called nitrogen mustard.

The father-daughter team worked together for three years until Louis died of a heart attack in 1952. Harlem Hospital asked the heartbroken Jane to stay on and become director of the Cancer Research Center in her father's place. Honoring her father's memory by carrying on his work, Jane experienced success with trials of triethylene melamine against lymphoma and alkylating agents against leukemia. *Mademoiselle* magazine gave her a 1952 Young Woman of the Year merit award "for her outstanding contribution to medical science with her evaluations of the efficacy of drugs in cancer treatment—evaluations that are now being translated, abstracted and quoted all over the world." She appeared to be rising fast in her field until, in December 1954, having just returned from presenting a paper at a research conference in Brazil, Wright learned she had been demoted.

The cause was a pair of grants awarded to the cancer research center from the U.S. government and the Damon Runyon Cancer Fund. Together the grants totaled $75,000, and they included a $9000 salary for the director of the center. All at once a white man, Dr. Alexander Altschul, was appointed director over Wright. The reason, hospital administrators explained, was that Wright was "too young and inexperienced" to handle a grant of that size. However, as another doctor pointed out anonymously to *The Amsterdam News*, "The board found it okay for Dr. Wright to head the project for two years after the death of her father when she was working free, but now when there is a salary attached, they want to take it away from her." The $9000 salary would have been higher than that of many staff members senior to Wright and might have led to envy. At the same time, many men junior to her were currently receiving a salary larger than hers, which was nothing at all. Although Wright never publicly complained about the demotion, it is very likely that her race and sex were both factors in the hospital administration's decision.

JANE WRIGHT IN THE LABORATORY, EBONY, 1961.
SOPHIA SMITH COLLECTION, SMITH COLLEGE.

The *Amsterdam News* raised so many questions about the change of positions on the grant that the mayor vowed to investigate, but there is no evidence that anything came of his promise. By 1955, the papers were reporting increased racial tension at the hospital, which now largely served a poor and black clientele. Harlem Hospital was overcrowded, understaffed, and less well funded than any other New York City hospital. Conditions did not improve, and in August 1955, Jane Wright resigned and moved to Bellevue Hospital of New York University. There she accepted a position as director of cancer chemotherapy and instructor of research surgery. Several of Harlem Hospital's cancer center staff went with her.

At Bellevue, Wright's center promptly received a new grant from the Damon Runyon Cancer Fund. In five months, she was appointed assistant professor of the associated N.Y.U. School of Medicine, and in 1961 she was made adjunct professor of research surgery. At Bellevue and N.Y.U., Wright continued her careful studies of new and experimental cancer drugs. She served patients who were dying and had no other hope. For each patient she tried one of the new drugs appearing from pharmacology laboratories. She carefully recorded dose, timing, side effects, and response, how the patient felt and whether the tumor shrank (a partial response) or disappeared (a remission). Among the most promising of the drugs she tested were mithramycin, which cured three of fourteen patients with deep, inoperable brain tumors, and methotrexate, which she proved to be helpful against breast cancer. In 1960 Wright also showed that methotrexate could send into remission a chronic and usually fatal cancer that was called mycosis fungoides because it looked like a purplish fungus growing in the skin.

In the late fifties Wright grew increasingly concerned about medicine's inability to predict what drugs might work on what tumors, even after the drug had been tested in animals. She wondered if testing samples of the tumor against drugs in the laboratory might help. Wright asked her surgical colleagues to give her a small sample of tumor tissue at the time of biopsy or surgery. Then she cut the sample into cubes one or two millimeters on a side and suspended them in a nutrient broth that allowed the cells to grow. Whenever she started a patient on a new drug, she also began treating the patient's cells with that same drug in the laboratory, using three different

PLAQUE OF MYCOSIS FUNGOIDES

*A rare type of T-cell lymphoma, **mycosis fungoides** begins as a rash, often itchy, that may look like unhealing eczema or psoriasis. The skin eventually develops plaques, or patches of thickened, inflamed skin that may break down. Skin biopsy can make the diagnosis. Although mycosis fungoides lingers for a long time in the skin, it eventually progresses to involve internal organs. A number of treatments may stabilize the disease or send it into remission. These include ointments or pills, ultraviolet light, local radiation or total skin electron beam radiation, among others.*

WRIGHT AT NEW YORK UNIVERSITY HOSPITAL, 1963

doses that had been standardized against a known cell line. After treating the cells for four days, Wright graded microscopic changes in the cells, classifying them into one of four grades of sensitivity against that particular drug. At the same time, she followed the patient's clinical response to the drug, adjusting the dose in case of toxicity and continuing the course of treatment for six to eight weeks.

Wright learned that when a drug had no effect on the tissue culture, it almost never worked in the patient. If a drug did shrink or destroy cancer cells in culture, it also worked in the patient seventy percent of the time. From Wright's observations in the laboratory she could even begin to make hypotheses about how each drug did its work. Following this multipronged approach, Wright created a kind of library for the rational choice of chemotherapy. She published numerous papers, becoming a nationally recognized expert on the choice, dosing, combinations, and timing of chemotherapy for a broad range of cancers.

In the 1960s, working with a team at N.Y.U. School of Medicine, Wright addressed another problem. Drugs effective against cancer were toxic to normal tissues as well. Wouldn't it be better if the drug could be delivered mostly to the cancerous tissue, bypassing the rest of the body? With Wright's advice, the surgical team connected, for example, an artery leading to a leg with a vein that drained that leg, and injected the chemotherapy drug into the newly connected vessel. That meant the drug passed by the tumor again and again, with relatively little of it escaping to affect the rest of the body. In 1964, Wright further improved this approach by developing catheters that could be threaded through an artery right to the tumor site, even in places difficult to reach by simple surgery, like the spleen, kidneys, or liver. Patients who received such localized perfusion of cancer drugs suffered fewer side effects and experienced some improvement in their symptoms. Still, the drugs, given to terminal patients, usually prolonged life by only a few weeks. One exception was a drug called actinomycin D, which appeared to cure three malignant melanoma patients entirely.

By 1964, Wright had become convinced that doctors caring for cancer patients, practicing the new specialty of oncology, required a better way of exchanging information and support. With six other doctors, all male, she founded the American Society of Clinical Oncology. That same year, President Lyndon Johnson appointed her to be one of two women on the President's Commission on Heart Disease, Cancer and Stroke. The commission advocated for better communication of research advances to doctors and hospitals, and its recommendations spurred the creation of a national network of specialized treatment centers to carry out clinical research and provide the best care. In 1967 Wright wrote,

> It is discouraging . . . to realize that the amount of money that goes into medical research in this country is astoundingly little compared to . . . the cost of a single day's war in Vietnam. The money made available for cancer research by the federal government amounts to some $170 million a year. Contrast this to the $553 million spent in the country for greeting cards, or the $358 million for chewing gum. If we can afford these things why can't we put enough money and enough people to work to solve the cancer problem?

Wright said at the time that if what was known about cancer treatment could be shared across the country, fifty percent of cancers could be cured. She also believed that many cancers might prove to be caused by viruses.

> *"People in medicine speak the same language, have one universal interest and a common goal."*

In the fifties, Wright's husband David Jones spent three years working in Ghana to establish the first life insurance company in western Africa's Gold Coast. In 1957, Wright arranged to visit Ghana on a medical mission. Four years later she led a trip to Kenya and Tanganyika, later called Tanzania, a year before they achieved independence. The visiting team camped out at night, often hearing lions roar in the distance, and treated patients during the day. Wright published a paper on her visit, concluding it by saying,

> *Cooperation through international medicine should do more than heal the ravages of disease, the common enemy of all peoples. It can help heal the tensions, misunderstandings and anxieties of the world—people in medicine speak the same language, have one universal interest and a common goal.*

In 1973, pursuing this ideal, Wright became vice president of the African Research and Medical Foundation. She also led medical delegations to China, Eastern Europe, and the Soviet Union, where the teams shared research and clinical findings with local doctors.

Despite working long hours, Wright maintained a strong family life. In her home community, people knew her as Mrs. David Jones or simply Jane Jones. Her two daughters followed the family tradition of accomplishment: Jane became a psychiatrist and Alison a clinical psychologist.

Although Wright never complained of racism affecting her own life, and although she did not follow her father into civil rights work, she did speak of racial politics within her own

By 2015, the combined five-year survival rate for the four biggest cancer killers in the United States was 58 percent, versus 25 to 30 percent in 1983, according to the American Cancer Society.

MOSAIC OF EMPRESS THEODORA OF BYZANTIUM, WHO DIED OF BREAST CANCER IN 548 C.E.

> *"Religion provides the moral and ethical basis of human rights.*
> *Government provides the needed protection under law."*

African-American community. On several occasions, she gave sermons in black churches. In 1962, speaking "On Human Rights, Human Dignity, and the State Law" at St. Luke's Methodist Church, she was frank about the problem of racism, saying, "The very violence of our times bespeaks the strength of the surge for true freedom and equality, as those who see their special privileges and dominant status threatened by this upward thrust, protest and attempt to block the march of history." In her sermon, Wright explained state antidiscrimination laws and the work of the State Commission for Human Rights, which exerted its effect primarily through education and persuasion of offending employers. She concluded with her customary optimism,

> *Here is one area of living in which Church and State work in unison toward their common goal. Religion provides the moral and ethical basis of human rights. Government provides the needed protection under law . . . True freedom and human dignity for all people is possible, if we have the inner strength and vision to live by our faith, not by our fears.*

In July 1967, Wright was invited to join the faculty of her alma mater, New York Medical College, as a full professor of surgery and an associate dean. It was the highest medical school position occupied by an African American woman up to that time. Proving to be an able administrator, she set up the medical school's new training programs on heart disease, cancer, and stroke. As she became more well known, Wright also received other awards and took on new duties. She received honorary doctorates from the Women's Medical College of Pennsylvania and Denison College. She became a trustee of Smith College and of the New York branch of the American Cancer Society, and she joined the editorial board of the *Journal of the National Medical Association.*

After her husband David Jones died of heart failure in 1976, Wright continued her research, teaching, and work in administration. In 1983 the National Medical Association asked her to give a lecture at their national convention. Wright spoke on "Cancer Therapy: Past, Present, and Future." She traced the history of cancer treatment from cautery—burning with hot metal—under the Egyptian Imhotep, to arsenic paste used by Hippocrates, to the current three-pronged approach of surgery, radiation, and chemotherapy. Being part of a long tradition of medicine was important to Wright. As she told a high school audience in 1982, "There is a deep satisfaction in knowing you are a part of a continuing process and program, that you have picked up where others have left off and others will pick up where you left off."

In 1987, Jane Wright officially retired. New York Medical College named her a professor emeritus. At last she had time to return to watercolor painting, sailing the waters near Fire Island, and

FAREWELL PARTY FOR JANE C. WRIGHT, GUANGZHOU, CHINA, 1986.
SOPHIA SMITH COLLECTION, SMITH COLLEGE.

reading her beloved mystery novels. She lived another twenty-six years, until she died in 2013 at the age of 93.

Jane Wright was atypical among African Americans raised early in the twentieth century for the advantages of class, material well-being, educational heritage, and opportunity she enjoyed. Largely avoiding racial barriers, Wright built a successful career in medicine as a pioneer in cancer chemotherapy. With 135 published papers and chapters in nine books, she helped create a specialty, made a substantial contribution to medical knowledge, and prolonged or saved the lives of many thousands of patients. Despite the deaths of so many patients she fought to save, she always remained optimistic. As she told one interviewer, "There is so much that is unknown in the field that there is a constant sense of adventure in my work." President of the American Society of Clinical Oncology Sandra Swain said of her, "Not only was her work scientific, but it was visionary for the whole science of oncology . . . It's amazing to me that a black woman, in her day and age, was able to do what she did."

Timeline | 1918-1962

1918 | British women win the vote

Birth of Rosalind Franklin | 1920

Cecilia Payne leaves for America | 1923

1923 | Death of Hertha Ayrton

MARY POPPINS
BY P.L. TRAVERS

P.L. Travers publishes | 1934
Mary Poppins

HERTHA AYRTON,
PHYSICIST

1938 | Enters Newnham College

World War II | 1939-1945

INDIAN STAMP

1945 | Receives PhD in
physical chemistry

Studies coal | 1946-1950
in Paris

1947 | Indian
Independence Act

England's National | 1948
Health Service is created

1950-1953 | Studies DNA in London

Takes Photograph 51 | 1952

Studies Tobacco Mosaic Virus | 1953-1957
structure

1953 | Watson and Crick publish DNA structure

Suez Crisis: Israel, Britain | 1956
France invade Egypt

1956 | Dorothy Crowfoot Hodgkin publishes
structure of Vitamin B12

Death of | 1958
Rosalind Franklin

DISABLED EGYPTIAN
TANKS DURING THE
SUEZ CRISIS

1960 | The Beatles
form a rock
band in
Liverpool

Watson, Crick, and | 1962
Wilkins win Nobel Prize

THE BEATLES

[156]

16 | *From Charcoal to Viruses*

Rosalind E. Franklin

1920-1958 | *England*

On May 2nd, 1952, Rosalind Franklin returned from a meeting of the Royal Society to her King's College laboratory to check on a DNA sample. Inside the X-ray diffraction camera that she had carefully set up with her graduate student Raymond Gosling, her sample of DNA fiber had switched from its "dry" form, which she called A, to its longer, more stretched out, "wet" form, B. After more than twenty-four hours of exposure, the resulting photograph was the finest Franklin had yet taken. A pattern of dark spots forming an X stood out against an unclouded white background, in the clearest proof yet that the molecule pictured was a helix. But Franklin already knew that, so she labeled the photograph "51" and set it aside. Then she returned to her perusal of the more complex A form of the molecule, whose photographs carried more detail and therefore, she felt, more information.

Eight months later, while Franklin was working hard to finish three scientific papers, a colleague she distrusted and disdained showed Photograph 51 to the young American scientist James Watson, who was working with Francis Crick to create a model of DNA. In his bestselling book *The Double Helix*, published years after Franklin's premature death, Watson wrote, "The instant

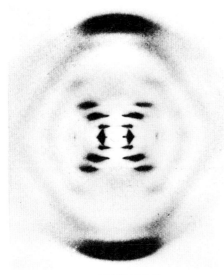

PHOTOGRAPH 51

I saw the picture my mouth fell open and my heart began to race." Only weeks later, Watson and Crick published their model of DNA structure in *Nature*. Franklin took their triumph in good spirit. She would like to have published first, but she was leaving King's College, where she had spent twenty-seven unhappy months, and she had already set her sights on other work.

Had Franklin known the truth about the poaching that set Watson and Crick on the right path, she might have felt less detached. Watson's unacknowledged look at her photograph led the pair to a Nobel Prize in which she had no share. More insidi-ously, Watson's later portrayal of her in his chatty, catty book established her in the public mind as a bad-tempered, insecure woman who not only refused to share data she couldn't interpret herself, but who didn't meet Watson's standards of feminine allure. The real shame is that the controversy over Photograph 51 has tended to obscure the fact that by the age of thirty-seven, Franklin made fundamental contributions to the understanding of coal and viruses as well as DNA. Her study of DNA was only one of three chapters in her scientific life, and the least happy one.

ROSALIND FRANKLIN

Rosalind Franklin was born into a wealthy, upper-middle-class Jewish family in London. The Franklin men were bankers and publishers, except for Rosalind's uncle, Herbert Samuel, who became High Commissioner to Palestine and a viscount. The family had servants and took summer vacations on the Continent. Franklin women were expected to make their mark in philanthropy, not by working for a living. Rosalind's conservative banker father, Ellis, had his own favorite charity: the Working Men's College, an evening institution meant to bridge the gap between the educated well-off and the uneducated working class. At the college, Ellis Franklin taught electricity, magnetism, and history, and held a number of posts, including vice principal.

Rosalind had three brothers, and she felt that her parents favored them. When she was nine years old, her parents sent her to boarding school, ostensibly to get her out of smoky London and into a more healthful environment. Rosalind believed it was to get her out of the way for the birth of her sister Jenifer, the Franklins' fifth child. Whatever the reason for her banishment, Rosalind did well at school, writing letters home about what she was learning in science and geography, playing hockey, and dutifully learning to sew.

At the age of eleven, Rosalind entered St. Paul's School, an academic day school near home. She played hockey, cricket, and tennis, and she performed at the top of her class, repeatedly win-ning scholarships, which her delighted parents returned so the money could be used by needier students. Rosalind joined the Debating Society, perhaps learning there to stand up and argue vehe-mently for her point of view. By age fifteen, she had determined that she wanted to be a scientist, so she concentrated on physics, chemistry, and mathematics. Serious and dedicated to her work, she never joined with her classmates in giggling gossip about schoolgirl crushes.

In the mid-1930s, as Rosalind finished prep school in England, Hitler was rising to power in Germany. By the time Rosalind, age seventeen and a half, sat for her entrance examinations to Cambridge University, Germany had annexed Austria. Rosalind passed with the highest examination marks in chemistry, winning another scholarship, and she accepted a seat for the fall at Newnham College, the second college for women at Cambridge. Meanwhile, she spent a couple of months in Paris perfecting her French. At home, her parents worked to help resettle Austrian Jewish refugees.

At Newnham College, Rosalind added mineralogy to her studies. For sport, she switched from hockey to squash. She wrote home often about lectures she attended, professors she clashed

FRANKLIN ON HOLIDAY IN NORWAY

with, and the strange indifference of Cambridge scholars to the disaster unfolding for the Jews of Europe. The summer she turned nineteen, the entire family took a holiday trip to Norway, only to flee home when the Nazi-Soviet non-aggression pact was signed on August 24, 1939. Britain was now approaching war with Germany, and Ellis Franklin wanted Rosalind to take a leave of absence from the university to contribute in some way to the war effort. She declined, and he relented. Rosalind spent her second year at university during the early, eerily quiet months of World War II. She and her friends were required to run for bomb shelters during a series of false alarms for German air raids that never materialized. But by the time her third year began, the war had come to England in earnest, with London suffering under the Blitz. Rosalind studied harder, focusing on crystallography and physical chemistry. She performed well enough on her final exams (university in Britain is normally three years long) to graduate with high honors and receive a research grant for graduate study.

For postgraduate research, Franklin was assigned to work on gas phase chromatography with Professor R.G.W. Norrish. It was an unfortunate assignment. Norrish's department had shrunk; he was drinking heavily; he had a low security rating and was barred from serious war work; and he took out his bitter disappointment on his underlings. He gave Franklin a meaningless project that she soon demonstrated could not be done in the way he prescribed. "When I stood up to him he became most offensive and we had a first-class row," she wrote. It was not the last time Franklin would clash with a supervisor who had lost her respect.

ELECTRON MICROGRAPH OF ACTIVATED
CHARCOAL

Activated carbon, *sometimes called activated charcoal, is a form of carbon that has been processed to have numerous small holes or pores. These holes hugely increase the surface area of the carbon. Other materials interact with this large surface and often adsorb, or stick to, the carbon molecules. Small regular pores also allow the carbon to act as a molecular sieve, sorting materials on the basis of their size.*

Emergency room doctors often give activated charcoal to people who have ingested poisons; the poisons adhere to the charcoal and pass through the body without being absorbed. Activated carbon also has wide environmental uses. It can help to filter water for drinking, purify air, or clean up a chemical spill. It can adsorb poisonous mercury from the outflow of incinerators or power stations. Pouring vodka or whiskey through a carbon filter will improve its purity and taste. People using gas masks, scuba equipment, and space suits all breathe through carbon filters.

After a year with Norrish, Franklin found a position at the British Coal Utilisation Research Association (BCURA), where she could do research that was important to industry and the war effort but would also propel her toward her PhD degree. She investigated the porosity and shrinkage of coal and charcoal subjected to different temperatures. Living in a flat with a friend, she became a volunteer air raid warden and took holidays camping and climbing in Wales.

In 1945, Rosalind Franklin, age twenty-five, received her PhD in physical chemistry. Half in jest, she wrote to her friend, French chemist Adrienne Weill, "If you ever hear of anybody anxious for the services of a physical chemist who knows . . . a lot about the holes in coal, let me know." She presented a paper on the pores in coal at the Royal Institution, where she stood up to point out the errors in another presenter's diagrams. Although she was right, Harry Carlisle, head of crystallography at Birkbeck College, commented, "Her characteristic of being forthright when she knew she was on firm ground sometime gained her enemies."

"I find infinite kindness and goodwill . . ."

With the help of her conference presentation and Weill's endorsement, in 1946 Rosalind Franklin obtained a position at the *Laboratoire Central des Services Chimiques de l'Etat* in Paris. Franklin became one of fifteen researchers working under Jacques Mering, a charming and brilliant crystallographer. In Mering's Paris lab, Franklin spent four happy and productive years as a respected member of a team. She became fluent in French, cooked, sewed, kept up with fashion, went swimming and dancing, participated enthusiastically in lunchtime discussions, and joined in group holidays hiking and climbing mountains. Her living accommodations were spartan, but she wrote home, "I find infinite kindness and goodwill among the people I work with." The only real complication was that she appears to have fallen in love with Mering, who was not only married but had a separate female companion. Although Mering was also attracted to Franklin and fond of her, he recognized that she did not have the temperament for a lighthearted affair.

At the *Laboratoire*, Franklin continued to study coal, investigating the density and structure of different forms, and why some carbons turned into graphite with heating while others did not. She discovered that carbon could act as a molecular sieve, allowing certain substances such as water to pass through under certain conditions. She soon became an international expert in the topic, and for the rest of her life she was often invited to conferences to talk about coal, charcoal, and graphite.

Because she was not a French citizen, Franklin could not keep her job in Paris forever. By 1950, Franklin, now the author of nine papers, was seeking a research position back in Britain. Dr. John Randall at King's College, London, offered her a three-year fellowship to look at X-ray diffraction of proteins in solution. Franklin accepted. By the time she moved, however, Randall had changed the focus of her research. She would now be studying "the structure of certain biological fibers," namely DNA. Randall went on to say, "As far as the experimental X-ray effort is concerned there will be at the moment only yourself and Raymond Gosling," a graduate student. Randall neglected to mention that another senior scientist, Maurice Wilkins, was also studying the X-ray crystallography of DNA. Thus, Randall set the stage for a fateful clash of personalities and ambition.

Franklin returned to England reluctantly, wary of its provincialism and hidebound tradition. England had not yet recovered from the war. Food was still rationed, and a bomb crater still scarred the yard of King's College. Franklin arrived at the college and began to set up equipment while Maurice Wilkins was on vacation. The misunderstandings began as soon as Wilkins returned. He thought she had been hired as his assistant, who would

Both France and Britain had been devastated by World War II. The French unified around the theme of Liberation and the necessity of rebuilding their nation. They established the Fourth Republic under Charles de Gaulle and put aside class struggle for the moment. Women gained the vote in 1945, but other than that they mostly returned to traditional domestic roles. The economy grew steadily in the years after the war. In philosophy and the arts, existentialism and the absurd grew popular.

The end of World War II left Britain nearly bankrupt as it tried to maintain a global empire and large armed forces. In 1947, Britain gave independence to India, and its empire gradually began to dissolve. The working people of Britain, who had contributed so much to the war effort, felt they deserved some reward, and in 1948 the National Health Service was created, offering free medical care throughout life. However, on the home islands, austerity and shortages persisted until at least 1950, and sweets were rationed until 1954.

BOMB CRATER IN LONDON, 1941

CHEMISTRY

be turning her work products over for him to interpret. But that was not what she had been told. Moreover, Franklin was not impressed with Wilkins, who was retiring, soft-spoken, and shy, a far cry from the brilliant and charming Mering. And Franklin's discomfort extended beyond one awkward personal relationship. King's College presented what today would be called a hostile working environment. Women were not allowed to dine in the college's Senior Common Room. As an upper-middle-class Jewish woman, Franklin felt out of place in the jokey atmosphere of King's, which was full of young, rowdy, lower- middle-class men whose social occasions were awash in beer. Here was none of the casual equality and respect Franklin had so treasured in Paris.

MAURICE WILKINS

Uncongenial as she found the working atmosphere, Franklin willingly applied herself to the problem at hand. She and Raymond Gosling assembled and tweaked their equipment, and she prepared the thin fibers of DNA Wilkins had obtained from a Swedish investigator. Franklin methodically varied the temperature and humidity of her samples until she made an important discovery: DNA takes two different forms depending on the level of humidity. Part of the reason previous investigators had struggled to get good X-ray diffraction photo-

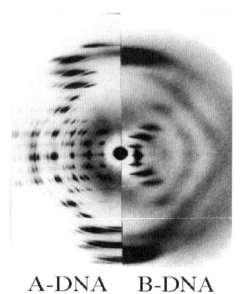

A-DNA   B-DNA

X-RAY DIFFRACTION IMAGES
OF DNA IN A AND B FORM

tographs of DNA was that their samples were a mixture of the two forms. Franklin presented her findings, along with her conclusion that the phosphate groups of DNA must be positioned on the outside of the molecule where they could easily take up water, at a conference in November 1951.

In the audience that day was Dr. James Watson, a brilliant young scientist recently arrived from the U.S. who was doing a research fellowship at the Cavendish Laboratory in Cambridge. Watson took no notes, but he rushed back to Cambridge to start building a model of the DNA molecule with his colleague, Francis Crick. They built a helix with three strands, and then invited Franklin and Wilkins, among others, to see it.

When she saw the Watson-Crick model, Franklin was incredulous at how ill-informed it was. Watson had misremembered her lecture and placed the phosphates on the inside of the helix, where they would not be able to absorb water in the way her research demonstrated. Franklin made her pointed criticisms and returned to London, convinced that building speculative models was a waste of time. Facts were what mattered. As for Watson and Crick, their embarrassed research boss, Dr. William Bragg, told them to leave DNA alone, and they turned their attention to RNA.

"Our dark lady is leaving us . . ."
–Maurice Wilkins

For the next year, Franklin continued taking her careful photographs, making measurements, and performing calculations. After one bitter argument between her and Wilkins, Randall, the laboratory chief, struck a compromise: Franklin should analyze form A of DNA, while Wilkins should analyze form B. It was a ludicrous solution, artificially dividing a problem instead of unifying a working group. Franklin grew ever more unhappy and defensive. She kept her data close. Sometime in the summer of 1952 she told Randall that she would be leaving his laboratory for a position at Birkbeck College. When Wilkins learned the news in November he was delighted, writing to Watson and Crick that "Our dark lady is leaving us next week." Knowing that Franklin was leaving and Wilkins would soon be supervising his PhD research, Raymond Gosling began to share with Wilkins more of the pair's work. Among the photographs he shared was their best image yet of DNA, Photograph 51.

Meanwhile, Franklin kept working. She didn't want to participate in some headlong race to discover DNA's structure: she just wanted to do good, careful science. She already knew that DNA was a helix, probably two-stranded, with phosphate groups on the outside and bases on the inside. She knew that the purine and pyrimidine bases existed in equal numbers, but had not yet reasoned out that they were paired. And she had not yet realized that the paired DNA strands of the helix ran in opposite directions.

Then, in January 1953, word came that Linus Pauling in California was claiming to have won the race to determine the structure of DNA. Watson and Crick were crushed until they procured an advance copy of Pauling's paper from his son, who worked at Cambridge. They saw at once that Pauling, misinformed by photographs much less clear than Franklin's, had repeated the mistakes of

WATSON AND CRICK WITH THEIR MODEL OF DNA

FRANCIS CRICK

their earlier model. It was at this point that Watson visited London and Wilkins showed him Photograph 51. He also pointed Watson toward Franklin's most recent research report to her funder, the Medical Research Council. From the report, Watson and Crick drew the key measurements they needed to build their model.

In the process of building their model, Watson and Crick had two critical insights. First, because he had seen the same phenomenon in horse hemoglobin, Crick realized from Franklin's data that the two strands of DNA must run in opposite directions. Second, the two managed to interpret the mysterious fact, demonstrated by Erwin Chargaff years earlier, that the number of adenosine subunits in DNA matched the number of thymine subunits, while cytosine's numbers matched guanine's. The only way this matching could happen, they realized, was if each set of two bases was paired, always occurring together. In fact, the base pairing could explain how a strand of DNA could replicate itself, by unzipping the helix and then allowing the cell to line up correctly paired bases in a new, matching strand. Like the negative of a print, each single strand of DNA would allow a strand identical to its first partner to be reproduced. When the old and new strands sealed together again, there would be two identical DNA molecules where once there had been one.

In April 1953, Watson and Crick hurried to submit a letter to *Nature* laying out their model. They invited both Wilkins and Franklin to submit companion papers of their own. Franklin's paper was titled "Molecular Configuration in Sodium Thymonucleate." In their own paper Watson and Crick referred generally to "unpublished experimental results and ideas of Dr. M.H.F. Wilkins, Dr. R.E. Franklin and their co-workers at King's College, London." They made no specific reference to the pieces of Franklin's work they had examined without her knowledge. Only in 1968, four years after receiving the Nobel Prize, did Watson reveal the source of their final inspiration. By then it was too late for Franklin to share in the glory.

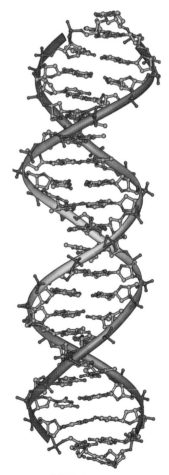

DOUBLE HELIX
STRUCTURE OF DNA

EFFECT OF TOBACCO MOSAIC VIRUS ON ORCHID LEAVES
FROM DEPARTMENT OF PLANT PATHOLOGY ARCHIVE,
NORTH CAROLINA STATE UNIVERSITY

By April 25th, when the three *Nature* papers appeared, Franklin had already moved to Birkbeck College. Birkbeck was much less well-equipped than King's, but the team Franklin joined was led by a man she respected, the legendary crystallographer J.D. Bernal, who had also been mentor to the accomplished crystallographer Dorothy Hodgkin. Bernal was a polymath, a Communist, and a proponent of sexual freedom. He had so many

affairs with co-workers that his secretary and a visiting researcher once started a very small and exclusive club of "Women Who Have Not Slept with Bernal." However, Bernal also truly liked and respected women, and finding no flirtatiousness in Franklin, he treated her with propriety as a skilled researcher and respected colleague.

At Birkbeck, Franklin focused on unraveling the structure of the tobacco mosaic virus, or TMV. TMV is an RNA virus that infects a wide variety of leafy plants, leaving them with mottled, brittle, and discolored leaves. Scientists were interested in TMV because it offered a model for how viruses

cause infection in general. Key to understanding that was determining its structure. Ironically, James Watson had also worked on TMV, during the period of his banishment from DNA. He had determined that the coat of the virus consisted of protein subunits arranged in a helix.

Franklin's office was on the fifth floor of an aging laboratory building, while her camera equipment was located in a leaky basement six floors below. As she waited to assemble her tools, she traveled to present papers on coal, first in Yugoslavia and then at a Gordon conference in New Hampshire, as part of her first trip to the United States. She lectured across America, from Woods Hole and Boston in Massachusetts to UCLA and Berkeley in California. She found Americans friendly but rather spoiled, "kind and well-meaning but incredibly ignorant and self-satisfied. On the other hand, the university scientists are as fine a crowd as I've met anywhere."

AARON KLUG

> *"She worked beautifully. Her single-mindedness made her a first-class experimentalist."*
>
> –Aaron Klug

Back in England, Franklin began to assemble her own research team. She became friendly with a researcher from across the corridor, a South African Jewish crystallographer and physicist named Aaron Klug. Klug decided to transfer to virus research in order to collaborate with Franklin. An excellent scientist, Klug later won a Nobel Prize in recognition of his work developing methods for electron microscopy of crystals and discerning the structure of protein-nucleic acid complexes. Together Franklin and Klug hired two graduate students, John Finch and Kenneth Holmes, both of whom went on to become Fellows of the Royal Society. Klug wrote of Franklin,

> *It takes imagination and intellect to know precisely what experiment to do, to design them, prepare the specimens and then to observe the results . . . She worked beautifully. Her single-mindedness made her a first-class experimentalist, with the sort of skill that blends intelligence and determination.*

Like Raymond Gosling, Franklin's graduate students were very happy to work for her. Holmes said he "would have gone through fire and water for her. She *was* prickly and difficult, especially at first, unable to put people at their ease," and very demanding about the quality of work done in the lab. But she could also be generous and thoughtful, and he admired her research. Others in the building found her standoffish and abrupt, but it didn't matter: she was the respected leader of a team doing high-quality work. She communicated and collaborated freely with, among others, James Watson and Francis Crick.

To further decipher the structure of TMV, Franklin began using a technique recently developed by crystallographer Max Perutz, in which she substituted atoms of a heavy element like mercury or lead into the virus protein. The new atoms changed the X-ray patterns found in photographs. Analyzing the differences revealed clues about the underlying structure. Using this technique, Franklin was able to determine that the RNA of the virus, instead of floating freely in its hollow core, was embedded in an interior groove between protein subunits in the winding wall.

Once they knew what components lay where, Franklin and her team built a model of the virus, using rubber handlebar grips from a

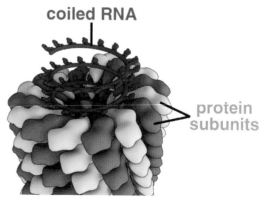

coiled RNA

protein subunits

STRUCTURE OF TOBACCO MOSAIC VIRUS

ROSALIND FRANKLIN IN TUSCANY

bicycle shop for the protein subunits. Later they were asked to build a much larger model for the Brussels World Fair. Meanwhile, Franklin and her team turned their attention to a whole variety of plant viruses.

Now at the top of her profession, Franklin traveled frequently to international conferences. She visited the U.S. again in 1956 on a tour paid for by the Rockefeller Foundation. People she met or stayed with on the trip found her warm, lively, and sunny. When visiting Caltech she took a side trip with scientific friends to climb Mount Whitney. She made the climb without difficulty, but a few days afterward, she experienced sharp pains in her lower abdomen. A doctor prescribed her painkillers and advised her to see her own physician as soon as she got home. Franklin was pleased not to have to interrupt her trip. On the way back across the country she visited her colleague and collaborator Don Caspar, a young American with whom she had developed a close friendship. Her biographer Brenda Maddox writes that "three women close to Rosalind believed she fell in love with Don Caspar that summer."

Back home once more, Franklin entered the hospital and underwent surgery that removed a malignant tumor on each ovary. A month later, she was back in the hospital for a total hysterectomy, removal of the uterus and what was left of her ovaries. She was thirty-six and mindful of the dangers of ovarian cancer, but she was also optimistic. No sign of cancer remained in her abdomen after the second surgery. For a time she recovered at her parents' house; then, wanting less fuss, she went to stay with Francis and Muriel Crick. For the first few months of 1957, she had energy enough for only half days at the lab. In April she was readmitted to the hospital with bleeding, and she started gamma radiation therapy. For the next year she worked whenever she could, insisting on walking the stairs from basement lab to attic office even when her graduate students offered to carry her. She lectured, built models, wrote papers, embraced every new therapy offered her, and refused to give up hope. But on April 16, 1958, Rosalind Franklin died. Her PhD students wept at the news. With characteristic thoughtfulness, she left enough money to her financially struggling research partner, Aaron Klug, to allow him to continue his research and fully launch his career. J.D. Bernal, in his *Times* obituary, wrote,

> She discovered in a series of beautifully executed researches, the fundamental distinction between carbons that turned on heating into graphite and those that did not . . . By the most ingenious experimental and mathematical techniques of X-ray analysis, she was able to verify and make more precise the illuminating hypothesis of Crick and Watson on the double spiral . . . She then made her greatest contribution in locating the infective element of the virus particle—its characteristic ribose nucleic acid.

Bernal went on to praise her gifts as a leader and organizer of research. Certainly her success as a team member in France and the leader of a team at Birkbeck College should go a long way toward debunking the idea that Rosalind Franklin was someone who could not or would not collaborate.

In 1962, the Nobel Prize in Physiology or Medicine was awarded to Frances Crick, James Watson, and Maurice Wilkins for elucidating the structure of DNA. Franklin could not be considered; the prize is not awarded posthumously. It can also be shared by no more than three people, so whether she would have been included even if she were alive is unclear. In his acceptance speech, Francis Crick briefly mentioned her work in X-ray analysis, but neither he nor Watson mentioned how much use they made of that analysis.

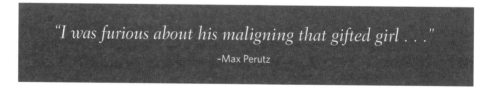

> "I was furious about his maligning that gifted girl . . ."
> -Max Perutz

The next time the world heard much about Rosalind Franklin was in 1968, when Watson published his popular book, *The Double Helix*. Rosalind's sister Jenifer calls the book "more of a novel than a factual account, unfair to Watson's colleagues and particularly unfair and hostile to Rosalind." Many of the characters portrayed in Watson's candid tell-all tale, including Wilkins, Crick, and Pauling, objected to the portraits of themselves they read in early drafts. They succeeded in getting some edits made. Not so Rosalind Franklin, who appears in the book as the ill-tempered, unimaginative, and unfeminine "Rosy." Others who knew Franklin reacted angrily. The molecular biologist Max Perutz wrote, "I was furious about his maligning that gifted girl who could not defend herself because she died of cancer." In part to disarm his critics, Watson added an epilogue stating that as a young man he had not fully understood the barriers a woman faced in science. However, he still failed to mention that in later years Rosalind Franklin was a good friend of the Cricks, or that Watson himself corresponded with her at length about virus structure.

Over the past fifty years, a more nuanced picture has emerged of Rosalind Franklin as a driven, gifted, sometimes difficult researcher who was capable of kindness and gaiety as well as stubborn taciturnity. She could be defensive and guarded when she felt belittled, but she thrived in free-wheeling, argumentative work groups with smart people who respected each other. She made fundamental discoveries in three areas of structural chemistry and biology, elucidating important findings about carbonaceous materials, DNA, and RNA viruses. Throughout her short career, Rosalind Franklin demonstrated courage, imagination, and a firm dedication to the truth.

CHEMISTRY

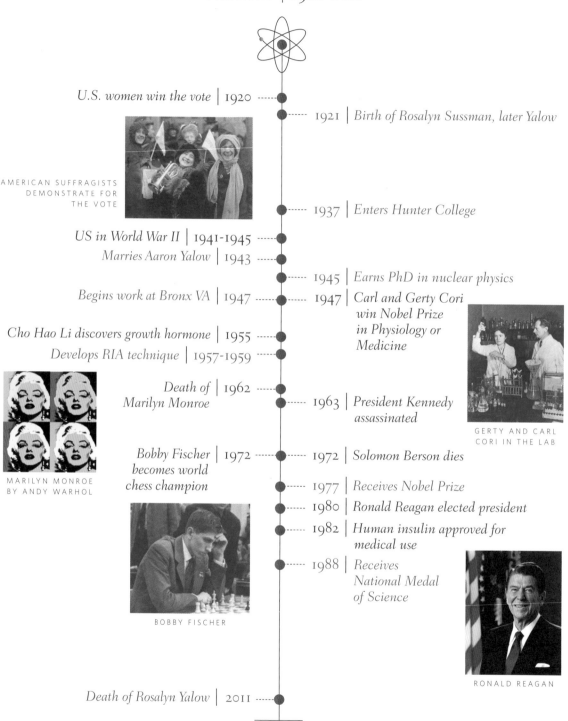

Timeline | 1920-2011

U.S. women win the vote | 1920

1921 | *Birth of Rosalyn Sussman, later Yalow*

AMERICAN SUFFRAGISTS
DEMONSTRATE FOR
THE VOTE

1937 | *Enters Hunter College*

US in World War II | 1941-1945
Marries Aaron Yalow | 1943

1945 | *Earns PhD in nuclear physics*

Begins work at Bronx VA | 1947   1947 | *Carl and Gerty Cori win Nobel Prize in Physiology or Medicine*

Cho Hao Li discovers growth hormone | 1955
Develops RIA technique | 1957-1959

Death of | 1962
Marilyn Monroe

1963 | *President Kennedy assassinated*

GERTY AND CARL
CORI IN THE LAB

MARILYN MONROE
BY ANDY WARHOL

Bobby Fischer | 1972   1972 | *Solomon Berson dies*
becomes world
chess champion

1977 | *Receives Nobel Prize*
1980 | *Ronald Reagan elected president*
1982 | *Human insulin approved for medical use*
1988 | *Receives National Medal of Science*

BOBBY FISCHER

RONALD REAGAN

Death of Rosalyn Yalow | 2011

17 | *Antibodies for Diagnosis*

Rosalyn Sussman Yalow

1921-2011 | *United States*

osalyn Sussman learned to read from her older brother Alexander before she entered kindergarten. Every week she and her brother made a trip to the public library to take out books. They lived in a Jewish neighborhood in the South Bronx where most adults had not graduated from high school. Their mother, Clara Zipper, an immigrant from Eastern Europe, had left school after the sixth grade. Their father, who ran a business selling paper and twine, had only an eighth-grade education. Still, both parents encouraged their children to aim for college.

Rosalyn was born on July 19, 1921. She remembered herself as being "a stubborn, determined child." When her first-grade teacher struck her with a ruler for some misdeed, Rosalyn grabbed the ruler and hit the teacher back. Most of the time, however, Rosalyn stayed out of trouble. When her brother was sick, she put on a homemade nurse's uniform and took charge of giving him medicine. When she needed braces, she earned money by doing piecework at home, helping her mother turn collars for a clothing factory. "If you wanted something, you worked for it," Rosalyn said. "It didn't keep me from doing my homework."

As children, most of Rosalyn's friends wanted to be scientists, but only Rosalyn was determined to marry and have children as well as to become a scientist. By seventh grade, she had chosen mathematics because she liked logical thinking. She excelled in school, and in junior high, after she competed three grades in two years, a teacher confided to her mother, "You know, your daughter is a genius." Mrs. Sussman was upset. She wanted a normal child.

Rosalyn attended a public high school for girls, where a science teacher inspired her to love chemistry. At fifteen, when she graduated from high school, her parents urged her to become a teacher. But Rosalyn still wanted to be a scientist. Her grades won her a place at Hunter College, the free but

THOMAS HUNTER HALL AT HUNTER COLLEGE

highly competitive public college for women that another Nobel Prize awardee, Gertrude Elion, had attended four years earlier.

The year after Rosalyn entered college, Eve Curie published her biography of her mother, Marie. Rosalyn found the book so inspiring—she saw in Marie Curie's persistence a reflection of her own stubbornness—that she began to consider majoring in physics. Her interest was sealed the next year when she "hung from the rafters" to attend a crowded colloquium given at Columbia by the nuclear physicist Enrico Fermi. Lise Meitner and Otto Hahn had just discovered nuclear fission, and Fermi explained fission in a way an eager young college student could understand.

Nuclear physics seemed to Rosalyn to be the most exciting subject in the world, where discoveries followed one another like falling dominoes, each one worthy of a Nobel Prize. There was one problem, however. Hunter College didn't offer a major in physics. Rosalyn lobbied to change that. Once her physics professor, teaching a class after lunch and wanting to keep his students awake, challenged them to find the two mistakes he would make in his lecture. Rosalyn Sussman found three. Still, because Rosalyn wore lipstick and went on dates, her two female physics professors at Hunter College disapproved of her, concluding she couldn't be serious about physics.

Rosalyn considered medical school, but as a Jewish woman, she knew her chances of being admitted were vanishingly small. Most medical schools had quotas for the number of Jewish students they would admit, and those few places went to men. Besides, she would never be able to afford the tuition. Instead, Rosalyn chose physics graduate school, reasoning that she could work as a teaching assistant to pay for her tuition.

But graduate schools, too, were largely closed to women, especially Jewish women. None of the schools Rosalyn applied to offered her a place. She had to find another way. Her professor Jerrold Zacharias helped her get a part-time job as a secretary to a Columbia biochemist, who told her she would be able to audit graduate classes. In the meantime, however, her employer insisted that she take a class in shorthand. It 1941, at age nineteen, the honors graduate in physics and chemistry enrolled in secretarial school.

ROSALYN SUSSMAN

Then, as it had for Gertrude Elion, World War II opened a door for Rosalyn Sussman. As young men were called up for the draft, graduate schools began to have trouble filling their classes. All at once the University of Illinois offered Rosalyn a teaching assistantship. "I tore up my stenography books," she wrote, but she stayed on at her secretarial job until June 1942. Then, before leaving for Illinois, she took two more summer courses in physics at New York University. She also broke up with her boyfriend, a law student who was not ready to commit to marriage.

> *"That A-minus confirms that women do not do well at laboratory work."*
>
> –Rosalyn Yalow's graduate school professor.

In Illinois, Rosalyn Sussman found herself the only woman in a department of four hundred physicists and engineers. She was the first woman to study in the physics department since 1917. Because of deficiencies in her undergraduate preparation, she had to take undergraduate physics courses along with her graduate courses, even while working half time as a teaching assistant. Determined to be a good teacher, she sat in on classes taught by a top-rate instructor "to learn how it was done." In her own class work, she performed excellently, receiving twenty-one As and one A-minus. The A-minus was in a laboratory class, and the professor wrote sourly, "That A-minus confirms that women do not do well at laboratory work."

On the first day of graduate school, Rosalyn met Aaron Yalow, the unassuming son of a rabbi. Like Rosalyn, Aaron studied nuclear physics, and the two of them shared a thesis advisor, Maurice Goldhaber. An Orthodox Jew who would not work on the Sabbath, Aaron was dedicated but less intense about his work than Rosalyn, who married him in June 1943.

In Maurice Goldhaber's lab, Rosalyn Yalow learned to construct and use apparatus for measuring radioactive substances. She was driven; Goldhaber remarked on her aggressiveness. When she graduated in 1945, she left Aaron behind to return to New York City to find a job. No university hired her, so she became the first woman engineer at a research laboratory for the International Telephone and Telegraph Corporation. A year later, when the IT&T research group disbanded, Yalow returned to Hunter College to teach pre-engineering courses to returning veterans and undergraduates. One of her Hunter students was Mildred Dresselhaus, who later became an eminent physicist at MIT. Dresselhaus reported that Yalow was the first person who suggested that she become a scientist. As for Yalow's class in modern physics, Dresselhaus called it "a very exciting class; it totally knocked me over." Yalow continued to mentor Dresselhaus for years after her graduation.

Aaron finished his PhD a year after his wife and joined her in New York. They took an apartment in Manhattan and then bought a small house in the Bronx. Aaron accepted a job in medical physics at Montefiore Hospital in the Bronx, and then later as a professor of physics at Cooper Union. But he was never as ambitious or hard-driving as Rosalyn. Some who knew the couple described Aaron as soft or weak compared to his wife. In reality, he was simply different. Religion was more important to him than physics. He was perfectly willing to stand in the shadow of his

FERMI AWARD WINNER MILDRED DRESSELHAUS, CENTER, IN THE OVAL OFFICE IN 2012.
OFFICIAL WHITE HOUSE PHOTO BY PETE SOUZA.

accomplished wife, offering help when needed. Though Rosalyn did the cooking and kept a kosher home for him, he accepted that she would be gone long hours at the laboratory and would never be a traditional housewife. He provided a sounding board for her ideas, and he encouraged her career. Choosing the right husband, Yalow would later tell female students, was a very important part of becoming a scientist.

In 1947, Aaron gave Yalow an important piece of advice. Hunter College had no research facilities, and working in a large government lab did not attract her. Aaron suggested she consider the new field of nuclear medicine. After volunteering for a few months at the medical physics laboratory of Dr. Edith Quimby at Columbia, Yalow found a consulting job at the Bronx VA Hospital. It was 1947. Nuclear reactors, no longer solely dedicated to building bombs, were creating the kinds of radioactive isotopes first discovered by the Joliot-Curies in 1933. Some researchers hoped these cheaper elements could replace radium for cancer treatment.

Yalow had something else in mind. She had read a book by physicist George Hevesy explaining how radioactive elements could be used as tracers. The elements decayed over time, allowing radioactive measurement of how they spread through the body. Yalow set up a radioisotope facility in a janitor's closet at the VA, and soon she was doing research full time. In two years she published eight research papers. Yet, as a female physicist in a culture where male physicians held sway, she soon decided she needed a physician on her team. She chose Solomon Berson, a young man with no research experience who was just finishing his medical residency. Like Yalow, Berson was Jewish and had faced prejudice in his career. It took him three years and twenty-one rejections before he was admitted to NYU Medical School. Berson could play chess against several people while blindfolded. He loved art and philosophy, and he sometimes shut himself up in the lab to play his violin.

After an interview where they worked through math puzzles together, Yalow decided he was the most brilliant man she had ever met.

After Berson joined the radioisotope laboratory in 1950, he and Yalow developed an unusually close research partnership. He taught her physiology and medicine; she taught him mathematics and physics. They conversed so intently that they could never be sure whose idea was whose; they finished each other's thoughts and took turns placing their names first on their research papers. To the outside world, Berson seemed the dominant partner. Yalow mothered him, made him tea and sometimes lunch, planned his travel, and carefully monitored institutional politics so she could advise him. Berson, with his charm and verbal agility, did most of the team's public speaking. But his respect for Yalow's scientific judgment was absolute. When discussing an experiment they challenged one another, questioning and fiercely debating, but always with respect. As Yalow related, "Neither Sol nor I had the advantage of specialized post-doctoral training in investigation. We learned from and disciplined each other and were probably each other's severest critic."

The team's first paper in *Science* explained their use of radioactively tagged cells to measure blood volume. Their technique was similar to that of ecologists who release tagged fish in a pond and then catch fish again to see what percentage are tagged. Suppose one out of a hundred fish the ecologists recatch is tagged. If the fish have mixed well, that means the number of fish in the pond is approximately one hundred times the number of tagged fish that were originally introduced. In the same way, by tagging a certain number of red blood cells and then drawing blood some time later, Yalow and Berson could closely estimate the number of red blood cells in the body.

In the early 1950s, Yalow and Berson studied the metabolism of albumin, a major protein in blood serum, and iodine, which is taken up by the thyroid gland. Then a diabetes researcher

BERSON AND YALOW IN THE LABORATORY

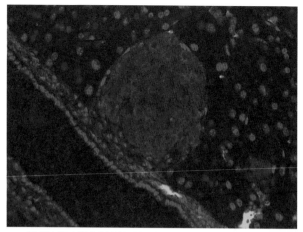

INSULIN-PRODUCING CELLS IN A MOUSE PANCREAS.
NUCLEI ARE BLUE; INSULIN IS RED.

named Arthur Mirsky asked them to test his hypothesis that diabetes was caused by an enzyme, insulinase, that degraded insulin too fast. The problem was of special interest to Yalow because Aaron was diabetic.

Yalow and Berson tagged insulin and injected it into volunteers. They found the opposite of what they had expected. Insulin lasted longer in diabetics than in people who had never used insulin before. And it wasn't just diabetics. At the time, insulin was sometimes used for shock therapy in psychiatric patients. It turned out that in these patients too—in anyone who had been given insulin before—insulin persisted in the blood longer than in unexposed people. But why?

Berson and Yalow hypothesized that patients developed an immune response to insulin, and that their antibodies latched onto the insulin molecule, making it harder to break down and excrete. This idea challenged the prevailing notion that a molecule as small as insulin could not evoke an antibody response. But the research team developed a method of paper chromatoelectrophoresis, in which a solution seeps into a sheet of filter paper while being drawn by an electrical current. The method allowed them to separate molecules by size. The radioactive label that they had attached to insulin migrated on the paper to the position expected for gamma globulins, or antibody molecules. This finding meant that the small insulin molecule was bound to much larger antibody molecules.

Still, the reviewers of the paper the pair submitted were unconvinced. *Science* rejected their paper; the *Journal of Clinical Investigation* accepted it on the condition that they remove the words "insulin antibody" from the title and text. But evidence supporting their discovery continued to accumulate. Some diabetics became resistant to insulin: the team showed that these patients had higher concentrations of anti-insulin antibodies.

As they worked on insulin, Berson and Yalow realized that they could use radioactive marking to measure hormones even in tiny amounts. This time they could do so without injecting any radioactivity at all into their subjects' bodies. The technique used antibodies, and they called it radioimmunoassay.

Radioimmunoassay works as follows. Researchers isolate a small amount of a hormone and inject it into guinea pigs or other animals, which form antibodies against it. The researchers

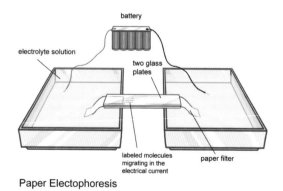

Paper Electophoresis

PAPER CHROMATOELECTROPHORESIS

harvest these antibodies and set them aside. Next they radioactively label a new batch of the hormone. Now they are ready to test a patient's serum. They mix the patient's serum with the antibody and the "hot," radiolabeled hormone. The hot hormone will bind to the antibody, but if there is hormone in the patient's serum, it will replace some of the hot hormone. By measuring how much radioactivity is bound to the antibody at the end of the process, researchers can determine how much unlabeled, "cold" hormone was in the serum sample.

Radioimmunoassay, or RIA, proved to be an astonishingly powerful tool for measuring biologically active molecules in tiny amounts. Antibodies are specific: they hold onto one kind of molecule and no other. And measuring radioactivity is much easier than trying to "see" molecules in any other way. In fact, RIA allows doctors to measure a trillionth of a gram of material in a milliliter of blood. That's like being able to find one particular person in 140 Earths full of people.

Following their invention of RIA in 1959, Yalow and Berson quickly used RIA measurements to make another key discovery about diabetes. They proved that there are two types of diabetes. In the first, which usually begins in childhood and is now called Type I diabetes, the pancreas stops making insulin. In the other, which usually begins in adulthood and is now called Type II diabetes, the body produces more insulin than normal, but the body's fat and muscle are relatively unresponsive to it.

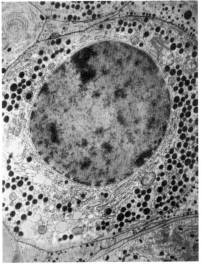

A HORMONE-PRODUCING CELL
IN THE PITUITARY GLAND,
FROM INFINITY-IMAGINED

*A **hormone** is a specialized signaling molecule secreted by a gland in a multicellular organism. This molecule is then carried by the circulation to distant organs where it interacts with a cell receptor, leading to change in the target cell's actions. Some hormones interact with surface receptor proteins. Others are transported to the target cell nucleus, where they affect the production of new proteins.*

Hormones are involved in digestion, burning food into energy, regulating growth and maturation, modulating moods, and preparing the body to fight or flee. Neurotransmitters are hormones that work widely throughout the body as well as in the brain, where they pass signals between connected neurons. Because hormones are exquisitely fitted to their receptor molecules, tiny amounts of them can have large effects.

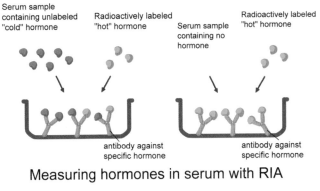

Measuring hormones in serum with RIA

RADIOIMMUNOASSAY

NATIONAL SOLDIER'S HOME IN
MILWAUKEE, BY JAMES STEAKLEY

*In 1812, the first U.S. Naval Home opened in Philadelphia to care for disabled veterans. A Soldiers Home followed 1853, and a hospital in 1855. In 1930, President Hoover created the **Veterans Administration,** and by 1947, there were 97 hospitals in the VA system. Major General John Hawley, director of VA medicine, worked to link these hospitals to medical schools and to bring medical residents and teaching fellows into VA hospitals. He also launched a program of research at VA hospitals that continues today.*

During these years of intensely productive research, Yalow grew her family. She had two children, Ben and Elanna. At the time, policy at the VA held that no pregnant woman could continue to work beyond the fifth month of pregnancy. But Yalow had made herself too useful to be dismissed. When Ben was born, she joked that she was the first woman to give birth to an 8 lb. 2 oz. baby after only five months of pregnancy. She went back to work a week later.

Rosalyn and Aaron moved to a house only a mile from the VA, so Rosalyn could slip home to fix lunch for the children. She did the same at dinnertime, rushing home to prepare a kosher meal and then often returning to the laboratory for a few more hours of work. Until Ben was nine, the family had live-in help; after that they used a series of part-time helpers. The Berson and Yalow families were close friends, but unlike Berson, with his chess and his violin, Yalow did not have hobbies. She worked and took care of her family.

> *"We were creating the competition."*

During the 1960s, Yalow and Berson spread the news about RIA. They trained visiting researchers in their laboratory—now grown well beyond the janitor's closet—and sent them home with valuable antibodies against hormones. Clinical laboratories began to understand the advantages RIA offered. Before, measuring insulin concentration in a diabetic had required a cup of blood. Now it could be done with a tenth of a milliliter. The method was quick, inexpensive, and adaptable. As Yalow wrote much later,

> *The current attitude is to keep things you discover secret, to keep others from learning so that you can exploit what you are doing to the maximum. We tried to train people in the use of radioisotopes in medicine. We tried to open the field of nuclear medicine. We weren't helping the competition; we were creating the competition.*

Yalow mothered the pair's few graduate students, demanding hard work from them but defending them fiercely against all scientific attack. She showed an unusual soft side when feeding the guinea pigs who produced antibodies for the laboratory. At their mealtimes she fed the guinea pigs lettuce, cuddled and kissed them and called them by name, although their names were only letters and numbers. She insisted that the personal attention made them more productive.

Then, in 1968, Berson took the position of chairman of medicine at Mt. Sinai School of Medicine. Yalow strongly urged him not to go. The politics of being an administrator, she said, would kill him. But Berson had a vision of building a relatively new medical school into a beacon of research-driven clinical excellence. Besides, he said, he would still come to the VA to do research.

After Berson's departure, Yalow became acting chief of the Radioisotope Service at the Bronx VA. She was also named a professor of medicine at Mt. Sinai, and later at Albert Einstein, Montefiore Hospital, and Yeshiva University in New York. But she continued to spend her time doing research at the VA. Berson remained loyal. In 1972, turning down an honor from the New England Diabetes Association, he wrote, "Dr. Yalow and I have been longtime collaborators, neither of us would consider accepting such an honor as this without the other sharing it."

GUINEA PIGS

But Yalow's warning proved prophetic. Tangled up in battles with a hospital administration that only wanted to increase clinical income, Berson found no time to continue his research. Worse, his health declined. In 1972 he had a mild stroke and spent some time at home. When he returned, he summoned a young Mt. Sinai physician, Dr. Eugene Straus, and instructed him to go work with Yalow at the VA. Under no circumstances, Berson instructed, was Straus to tell Yalow about the stroke. Straus did as he was told, but a few months later, Berson died of a heart attack at the age of fifty-three. Yalow was inconsolable. At his funeral she burst into tears and could not stop sobbing, to the amazement of all those who knew her reputation for toughness. Indeed, Yalow was devastated for over a year.

For a period after Berson's death, Yalow, at the age of fifty-one, considered going to medical school herself. Eventually, though, her confidence in her own knowledge returned. She asked the VA to rename the RIA laboratory after Berson so that his name would still appear on all research emanating from the facility. Then she went back to work. Some in the research community had considered Berson the real brains behind their partnership. Yalow set out to enlighten them. She worked a hundred hours a week, training Straus to play some of the role that Berson had. She proved that RIA could differentiate between insulins from pigs, dogs, and whales as well as humans. She showed that cholecystokinin, a gut hormone that helps digest fat in the small intestine, also works to transmit signals in the brain. The laboratory produced papers on ACTH (adrenocorticotrophic hormone) and growth hormone. In all, between 1972 and 1976, the Solomon Berson Laboratory produced sixty new papers. Meanwhile, Yalow also took over Berson's editing and public speaking roles. In 1975, Yalow was elected to the National

YALOW IN HER LAB

Academy of Sciences. In 1976, she became the first woman to receive the Lasker award for basic medical research, an award often considered a precursor to a Nobel Prize. Then, on October 13, 1977, Yalow received the phone call she had been awaiting. She had been awarded the Nobel Prize in Physiology and Medicine, the second American woman to be so honored. Yalow broke out the champagne.

Rosalyn and Aaron flew to Stockholm straight from their daughter Elanna's wedding in California. At the Nobel banquet, the student sent to walk Dr. Yalow to the platform mistakenly perched to wait on the wrong side of the table, behind Dr. Aaron Yalow. Wearing a long blue gown, Rosalyn Yalow stood and walked herself toward the podium, until the student caught up with her as she whispered a few forgiving words in his ear.

After the Nobel Prize, Yalow continued to work in her VA lab for another fifteen years. In 1976 she was excited to host a five-part PBS series about her heroine, Marie Curie. In 1988, President Reagan awarded her the National Medal of Science, the nation's highest honor in science. Although generous with her students, she remained intensely competitive. Yalow continued to critique others' work in the combative style she had developed debating Berson. Sometimes the clashes seemed to become personal. She mourned the increasing bureaucracy and regulation of science, objecting when regulators required her to separate her rabbits from her guinea pigs.

After retiring in 1991, Yalow became a spokesperson for the importance of science. She was still outspoken. She argued that the public's fear of small amounts of radiation was unwarranted. Once, when she spoke in favor of nuclear reactors at the Bronx High School of Science, the students booed her. Yalow spoke out against what she perceived as anti-science, anti-progress activism in the United States. Science, she pointed out, had increased the average lifespan of Americans by thirty years since 1900. She argued that women could succeed at being both mothers and scientists, saying, "It's a tragedy for society when talented women do not have children." She lobbied universities to provide daycare facilities so their child-bearing faculty could continue to work.

Meanwhile, RIA continued to make possible key advances in medicine. Today RIA is used to test the effectiveness of hepatitis treatment. It is used to test for underactive thyroid glands in newborns so that babies can receive supplements to save them from mental retardation. RIA detects drugs in the urine of cheating athletes or relapsing addicts. It allows the detection and treatment of a broad range of disorders in the endocrine system. It helps diagnose fertility problems so they can be treated. It allows blood banks to ensure that donated blood is safe.

Journalists occasionally asked whether Yalow regretted that she and Berson had never patented the RIA process. She answered, "Patents are about keeping things away from people for the purpose of making money. We wanted others to be able to use RIA."

At 87, Rosalyn Yalow suffered a stroke that left her clumsy on her right side. Still, she continued to go to the VA until a fall immobilized her. She died on May 30, 2011 at the age of 89.

> *"We must match our aspirations with the competence, courage, and determination to succeed."*

Yalow was brilliant, stubborn, competitive, and determined to have a life that combined science and family. The words of her Nobel Prize acceptance speech could serve to speak for all the women in this book.

We still live in a world in which a significant fraction of people, including women, believe that a woman belongs and wants to belong exclusively in the home; that a woman should not aspire to achieve more than her male counterparts and particularly not more than her husband. Even now women with exceptional qualities for leadership sense from their parents, teachers and peers that they must be harder-working, accomplish more and yet are less likely to receive appropriate rewards than are men . . . We cannot expect in the immediate future that all women who seek it will achieve full equality of opportunity. But if women are to start moving towards that goal, we must believe in ourselves or no one else will believe in us; we must match our aspirations with the competence, courage and determination to succeed; and we must feel a personal responsibility to ease the path for those who come afterwards.

FURTHER READING

Bret, Patrice and Brigitte Van Tiggelen. *Madame d'Arconville*. Paris: Hermann Éditeurs, 2011. This volume, written in French by multiple authors, is the first book-length study of the prolific Enlightenment author.

Fulhame, E. *An Essay on Combustion, with a View to a New Art of Dying and Painting, wherein the Phlogistic and Antiphlogistic Hypotheses are Proved Erroneous*. London: 1794. A recent facsimile edition of Mrs. Fulhame's lively essay is now available from Amazon and other sellers.

Levi-Montalcini, Rita, and Luigi Attardi. *In Praise of Imperfection: My Life and Work*. New York: Basic Books, 1998. Highlights Levi-Montalcini's determination, as well as the personalities of her friends, family, and colleagues.

Maddox, Brenda. *Rosalind Franklin: The Dark Lady of DNA*. New York: Harper Perennial, 2003. A thoughtful and balanced biography highlighting Franklin's scientific work and relationships with fellow scientists.

Mazzotti, Massimo. *The World of Maria Gaetana Agnesi, Mathematician of God*. Baltimore: Johns Hopkins University Press, 2007. This is a scholarly work that places Agnesi in her social, mathematical, and religious context.

McGrayne, Sharon. *Nobel Prize Women in Science: Their Lives, Struggles, and Momentous Discoveries*. New York: Joseph Henry Press, 2001. Well-written chapters about fourteen women, including six in this book, with equal attention to their personal lives and their scientific contributions.

Osen, Lynn. *Women in Mathematics*. Cambridge: MIT Press, 1975. Émilie Du Châtelet, Maria Gaetana Agnesi, and Sophie Germain are among the women mathematicians, primarily European, whose work and lives are profiled in this book.

Payne-Gaposchkin, Cecilia and Katharine Haramundanis. *Cecilia Payne-Gaposchkin: An Autobiography and Other Recollections.* Cambridge: Cambridge University Press, 1996. Contains Payne-Gaposhkin's brief and witty autobiography, *The Dyer's Hand*, along with biographical essays by her daughter and fellow astronomers.

Sharp, Evelyn. *Hertha Ayrton, a Memoir.* London: E. Arnold, 1926. An affectionate memoir by a friend, this book presents Ayrton as scientist, inventor, and suffragette.

Strohmaier, Brigitte and Robert Rosner. *Marietta Blau, Stars of Disintegration: Biography of a Pioneer of Particle Physics.* Riverside: Ariadne Press, 2007. A useful account of Blau's life, work, and historical context.

Taussig, Helen and Joyce Baldwin. *To Heal the Heart of a Child.* New York: Walker Publishing Company, 1992. Written for ages twelve and up, this is the only full-length biography of Helen Taussig, the pioneer of pediatric cardiology.

Zinsser, Judith P. *Émilie Du Châtelet: Daring Genius of the Enlightenment.* New York: Penguin Books, 2007. Readable and rich in period detail, this book nevertheless sticks to the facts.

GRAPHIA
MVNDANI
MAICI.